The Civilization of the American Indian Series

CROWFOOT

CHIEF OF THE BLACKFEET

CROWFOOT

BY HUGH A. DEMPSEY
FOREWORD BY PAUL F. SHARP

NORMAN
UNIVERSITY OF OKLAHOMA PRESS

CHIEF OF THE BLACKFEET

Dempsey, Hugh Aylmer, 1929–
   Crowfoot, chief of the Blackfeet.

   (The Civilization of the American Indian series, v. 122)
   Bibliography: p. 217
     1. Crowfoot, 1830–1890.   2. Siksika Indians.
3. Kainah Indians. I. Title. II. Series.
E99.S54C73   970.3 [B]   72–865

Crowfoot: Chief of the Blackfeet is Volume 122 in *The Civilization of the
American Indian Series.*

To my wife, Pauline (Apsuikaiaki)

FOREWORD

BY PAUL F. SHARP

This biography of a great Indian leader of the Canadian-American West is a welcome addition to the growing bibliography on North American Indians. Timely in its emphasis upon the life and character of a leader who devoted his life to the welfare of his Blackfoot people, it is equally valuable as a careful analysis of a diplomat and peacemaker who led his people through the perilous times that transformed them from nomadic hunters to reservation farmers, ranchers, and miners in western Canada.

Crowfoot will be better known among historians as a result of this book. More important, his contributions as orator, peacemaker, and diplomat restore a balance of perspective upset by the traditional emphasis upon the warlike Sitting Bulls, Poundmakers, and Crazy Horses of popular history on both sides of the forty-ninth parallel.

This biographical study is also a survey of the turbulent period on the northern plains in the decades from 1860 to 1890. While many Indian leaders called for war to resist the white man's greed, injustice, and callousness, Crowfoot sought cooperation and peace. He curbed his fierce warrior's resentment because he understood the strength of white society and clearly saw what so many of his fellow chiefs ignored: the only real choice facing his people was annihilation or domination by white governments. Completely loyal to his own people, he thus called for loyalty to the Queen's government and skillfully avoided involvement in the tragic and costly outbreaks that so often brought reprisals upon neighboring tribes. His loyalty to the government during the Riel Rebellion in 1885 captured the attention of Eastern newspapers, making him something of a hero and capturing the imagination of politicians and citizens alike. Romantics believed this loyalty grew out of an affection for the Crown and a respect for the redcoated justice of the Northwest Mounted Police. Realists, such as Father Lacombe, understood that he worked for peace because of a shrewd appraisal of self-interest.

Crowfoot embraced the doctrine of "one law for all people" in the Canadian West. In marked contrast to experiences south of the international boundary, where law enforcement rested in the hands of local citizens and population pressure ignored federal regulations, Crowfoot's efforts to preserve peace and to lead his people into a new era were rewarded. There is both sadness and hope in the picture of the one-time warrior, hoe in hand, working in the fields as an example to his people.

Hugh Dempsey has given us an intimate portrait of a great leader who devoted his life to his people. He also has written a convincing biography of a peacemaker who risked his life for his beliefs and deserves the reputation he earned as "father of his people."

PREFACE

Crowfoot was the leading chief of the Blackfeet during a turbulent twenty-year period which saw the disappearance of the buffalo herds, the signing of treaties, starvation, rebellion, and the beginning of a new kind of life under the yoke of the white man. Because of his skillful leadership and his propensity for peace, Crowfoot was lionized during his lifetime as a great friend of the whites, a man who was a loyal subject of Queen Victoria. Yet how could such a man be acceptable to the warlike Blackfeet? Was he nothing more than a government lackey, or was he something more than a "good" Indian?

Research for this book began in an effort to find the answer to these and other questions, for, although Crowfoot's name was well known, the events that had made it so were those few exciting adventures which made him look like a friend of the whites. In reality, Crowfoot was a strong leader whose only goal in life was to provide for his people. He had only one loyalty—to them.

The search for information about Crowfoot produced many surprises. The first was that, while he was a great Blackfoot chief, he was not a Blackfoot Indian. Rather, he had been born to the Blood tribe and had moved north to the Blackfeet when his widowed mother married a man from that tribe.

But perhaps the biggest surprise was the degree of Crowfoot's greatness. Some people, including a few Indians, had felt that he was essentially a weak man who had been under the dominating influence of such white men as Father Albert Lacombe and Colonel James F. Macleod. This study showed just how little control any white man had over the chief.

Another story which proved false was that Crowfoot had been a nobody before the coming of the North West Mounted Police in 1874. Fur trade and missionary records, as well as interviews with elderly Indians, showed that Crowfoot had been a prominent warrior and through his own abilities had become chief. As early as 1866, fully eight years before the arrival of the police, he was mentioned in fur trade journals as being an important leader.

More than anything else, however, research showed what a burden could be placed upon a man from a primitive society. In two decades, Crowfoot had to lead his people from familiar buffalo-hunting practices into an alien life dominated by Indian agents and reserve boundaries. That he did so without bloodshed, even in the face of shallow hypocrisy and incredible callousness, is a tribute to his strength. That he could do so with pride is a small measure of his ability.

Research on Crowfoot was started in 1957 and was carried on at intervals, using a variety of sources, including interviews with elderly Indians. The most helpful Blackfoot informants were Mrs. Jennie Duck Chief, Ayoungman, One Gun, Heavy Shield, Joe Crowfoot, and Mrs. Many Guns. From the Bloods were John Cotton, Bobtail Chief, and Jack Low Horn. Assisting in all these interviews was my interpreter and father-in-law, Senator James Gladstone. His excellent knowledge of modern English and old-time Blackfoot was of immeasurable value. Without his help and that of Indian informants, this book would not have been possible.

Thanks are extended to Lucien and Jane Hanks for providing me with copies of interviews they made with the Blackfeet in 1939 and 1941. While gathering data for their book *Tribe Under Trust*, they interviewed a number of old people who died within the next few years. Among them were Buck Running Rabbit, Duck Chief, and Many Guns.

Much valuable assistance also was given by the fathers of the Oblate Order, Edmonton, whose excellent archives contain much information on the early West. For other help I am grateful to Pat McCloy, Glenbow-Alberta Institute librarian, and John C. Ewers, of the Smithsonian Institution, Washington, D.C., who has been a friend and adviser for many years and has read this manuscript for me.

The illustrations appearing in this volume, unless otherwise noted, are from the collections of the Glenbow-Alberta Institute, Calgary, and are printed here with their kind permission. The Institute, which is my employer, has been most co-operative in making it possible for me to carry out this study.

This book has been published with the help of a grant from the Humanities Research Council of Canada, using funds provided by the Canada Council.

HUGH A. DEMPSEY

Calgary, Alberta

CONTENTS

ILLUSTRATIONS

MAPS

CROWFOOT
CHIEF OF THE BLACKFEET

A BLOOD BABY

The young man's name was Packs a Knife, *Istowun-eh'pata*, and his wife was Attacked Toward Home, *Axkyahp-say-pi*. They were neither rich in horses nor influential in the tribe, but in that year of 1830 they both were very happy, for their marriage had been blessed by the arrival of a fine baby boy.[1]

Packs a Knife and his wife were Blood Indians—a part of the nation the white traders called "Blackfeet" but which the Indians themselves called *Nitsitapi*, the Real People. There were three tribes in the nation, all speaking the same language. To the south were the Piegans with a population of about seventy-five hundred, while north of them were the Bloods and the Blackfeet, each with about forty-five hundred. Allied to the nation, but speaking in different tongues, were the Atsinas, or Gros Ventres, to the east and the tiny Sarcee tribe to the north.

These tribes ranged over the northern plains from the Upper Missouri River to the North Saskatchewan and from the Yellowstone River to the Rocky Mountains in search of food. Straddling the International Boundary between the land of the British Hudson's Bay Company to the north and the United States to the south, they recognized no allegiance except to their tribe and their land. The British traders were acceptable as long as they stayed on their own side of the Saskatchewan River, but the Americans, whether trappers or traders, had

---

[1] Although several dates have been given as the year of Crowfoot's birth, the most reliable source is a letter from Indian Agent Magnus Begg to the Indian commissioner, January 10, 1889, which gave the chief's age as fifty-nine. In Selected Papers from Blackfoot Indian Reserve, 1883–1892, in author's possession.

3

been despised ever since the Lewis and Clark expedition had killed one of the Blackfoot people. Anyone coming from the south was considered an enemy.

At the time of the baby's birth, the Bloods were camped in one of the many bottoms along the Belly River in the middle of their hunting grounds. In the parents' own little camp, the leader was Crying Bear, a great warrior, medicine man, and older brother of Packs a Knife.[2] The chief of the whole tribe was Bull Back Fat, a respected leader who in the following year made peace with the American traders after twenty-six years of warfare.

The young child, whose future destiny lay not with the Bloods but with the Blackfoot tribe, was given the name of Shot Close, or *Astoxkomi*. This was his baby name and would remain with him until he was given one or more titles of manhood. Names were not just a means of identification; they were family possessions, considered to be living things that floated homelessly in the air when their owners died. So a name remained within a family, being passed down to a nephew, son, or other relative when he performed some heroic act which entitled him to such an honor.

In the days and weeks that followed, Shot Close's life was like that of any Blood baby. He was fed, he was packed on his cradle board, and, like young and old, he traveled. In summer the camps gathered for the holy Sun Dance in the shadow of the Belly Buttes; from there the Indians drifted onto the plains in search of buffalo. By autumn, their travois loaded with pemmican, they followed the herds north and picked good camping places where they would be protected from the howling blizzards and the ever-drifting snow. Some went to the

---

[2] In Blackfoot, the word *ne'sa* may be translated either as "uncle" or "older brother." There are many such problems with kinship terms. For example, the word for "brother" may refer to a half-brother, adopted brother, stepbrother, or, in some cases, a cousin or nephew.

Belly River, some to the seclusion of the Porcupine Hills, and others north to the Spitzee River.

They were not concerned about the white man, for his presence was felt only through his trade goods and his diseases. Although the Hudson's Bay and North West companies had opened trading posts on the northern fringes of Blackfoot hunting grounds as early as 1790, no fort had survived within their country for more than a few months. And, unlike their Cree neighbors, the Blackfeet had not changed their way of life to suit the traders.[3] They were buffalo hunters and offered dried meat and horses in exchange for weapons, utensils, beads, and blankets. The traders needed meat to provision their northern outposts and horses for their transportation systems, so they made no attempt to turn the Blackfeet into trappers and beaver hunters. Rather, they left them alone and did not interfere with their tribal systems, religion, or customs.

So passed the months.

The baby grew, took his first faltering steps, and became a toddler. He graduated from the moss bag and took a bumpy place on the travois. There, nestled among the family's compact possessions, he saw the long lines of the moving camp, the prairie covered with black herds of buffalo, the dust-ridden sky which fell away to clear blue and finally dropped behind the jagged line of the Rockies.

Although he did not understand it, he saw his father ride away from camp, his face painted with vermilion. He heard his mother pray and watched her anxious face as the days passed in their lonely lodge. And he saw the moment of joy and the hours of rejoicing when the father and his comrades returned with their herd of enemy ponies. These things he saw and, although he did not understand them, he felt the

3 Although the term "Blackfeet" is used here, "Blackfoot" is the official name now used by the Canadian government.

5

surging emotions of the people around him. He was too young to realize that a day would come when he too would ride out from camp in search of glory and victory.

When Shot Close was a little more than two years old, a baby brother joined the family. Packs a Knife was now blessed with two sons, who would be warriors and hunters of the Blood tribe. The second son, whose boyhood name now is forgotten, later took the name of Iron Shield, *Mexkim-aotan,* and then became known as Chief Bull, *Ninastumik.*

Several months after the birth of this second baby, Packs a Knife again went to war. This time it was to raid the Crows, who were enemies of all the Blackfoot nation. They lived far to the south, along the Yellowstone River, and were known for their fine horses. Again Packs a Knife painted his face and rode out with his comrades. Again he disappeared over the ridge of the valley and toward the southern horizon.

But this time he did not return.

There was pitiful wailing in the camp when the survivors returned. Instead of finding the Crows in their usual camps, the Bloods had been ambushed and several of the party killed.[4] Among those who died was Packs a Knife, the young man who wanted horses for his family and honor for his tribe. A man with a wife and two small boys.

Grief-stricken, Attacked Toward Home moved to the lodge of her father, Scabby Bull, slashed her arms and her legs, hacked off her hair, and painted her face in mourning. Her two children, frightened and confused, stayed close to their grandfather and watched as their mother went daily to a nearby hill and wailed for her husband who would never return.

There was sadness in their lodge for many months; but life was harsh among these people, and death was a part of living.

[4] Information provided by Heavy Shield, Blackfoot Indian, in an interview, March 8, 1957.

Warriors died in battle, women died in childbirth, children
died of hunger and disease. Death was the ever-present enemy
which took away their people to the Sand Hills far to the east.
There they lived a shadow existence where there was no happiness, no sadness.

The period of mourning passed, the scars of the flesh healed,
and the hair grew long again. A peacefulness settled upon the
lodge, and Scabby Bull settled down to the task of teaching
Shot Close the lessons and responsibilities of a warrior and
hunter. He told the legends of his tribe, many of them carrying
lessons for the young listener, and he told the boy what would
be expected of him as he grew older.

By the time he was five, Shot Close had been released from
the clumsy seat on the travois and had his own place behind
his mother on the pony. His chubby legs could barely straddle
the horse, but he thrilled to its rhythmic gait as they traveled
from place to place in the constant hunt for food.

One day they were camped on the Belly River when Shot
Close saw a party of strangers enter the valley. They were not
Bloods, yet they spoke the language of the Real People. Their
faces were painted as his father's had been, and before them
they drove a herd of captured ponies. As they came to the
camp, they sang their victory song. Uncle Crying Bear went
to greet them and learned they were men of the Blackfoot
tribe, most of them from the Biters band, and had just returned from raiding the Crows. They were invited to stay with
the Bloods until they learned where their people were camped.

It was a pleasant stay. The buffalo were plentiful and the
warriors were treated well as they mixed with their allies.

A visitor to the lodge of Scabby Bull was a young warrior
called Many Names, *Akay-nehka-simi.* Although his first visit
may have been to see the old man, he soon was attracted by
the young widow and remained with the Bloods long after his

7

comrades had returned to their home camp. Shot Close paid little attention to the stranger, for these were the years when his grandfather was the center of his life, as the old man taught him to ride and shoot and recounted the tales of warriors, spirits, and supernatural creatures. However, it was no surprise to the old man when Many Names tied his captured horses before his lodge as an indication that he sought the hand of his daughter.

Attacked Toward Home was flattered by the attentions of the Blackfoot warrior and knew that she cared enough for him to be his wife. But there was a problem, for her father's whole life centered around Shot Close. It was a difficult decision, but at last she agreed to leave the older boy to be raised by her father, while she took Iron Shield with her and her new husband. It was settled. The elder boy would remain a Blood Indian, and the younger would be adopted by the Blackfeet.

Shot Close was not consulted about this arrangement and, when he saw his mother and younger brother riding away with the stranger, he did not like it. He was only five years old, but he was a determined boy. As quickly as his short legs could carry him, he began trotting along the trail after his mother. The travois and horses traveled slowly, for they carried all the family's belongings, but it was many hours and many miles later before the little boy caught up with his mother. They were out on the prairie, far from camp, with no one to take him home again.

"Let's go back with the boy," sighed Many Names.[5] Scabby

5 When a native informant has proved to be reliable and uses actual conversations in his narrative, these are reproduced. The Blackfoot language is a spoken one and much of the history and folklore is passed down from generation to generation in such a form that one would think the teller of a hundred-year-old tale actually had witnessed the event. The conversations when compared with actual records often show a remarkable degree of accuracy. A good example is the Blackfoot Treaty of 1877, about which some modern informants who speak only in their native tongue have been able to

8

Bull would be worried when he found the child was gone and the old man already was unhappy over seeing his daughter leave. When they got back to the Blood camp, Shot Close was determined to stay with his mother, while Scabby Bull insisted that the boy remain with him. At last Many Names made a suggestion.

"Rather than bringing sadness to the family," he said to Scabby Bull, "why don't you come too, and we'll all stay together." So Scabby Bull went to the Blackfeet and remained with them for the rest of his life.

So did Shot Close, the young boy who almost was raised as a Blood. But Fate had planned a different life for him in another tribe, and love for his mother had started him toward this goal.

When the camp was struck, the little party moved out from the wooded valley and onto the sweeping plain. In the lead was Many Names, the Blackfoot, while behind him followed his new family—a wife, two children, and a father-in-law. Over the plains and past the Little Bow River they went until they found the main trail north from Ghost Pound Creek. It was well rutted from travois poles cutting deep into the soil. The trail, leading across the arid flats, touched all the best springs along the route. Past the Little Bow and into the sand-hill ridges it went until at last it dropped into the wide valley of the Bow River.

The Bow was a wide and treacherous stream, but the crossing was defined clearly by a stony ridge that extended from one bank to the other. In low water a man could step from stone to stone along the ridge and never wet the soles of his

pass on conversations which are not unlike those recorded in Morris's *Treaties of Canada*. While there may be variation in the actual wording, the essence of such speeches remained the same. For this reason, one is not necessarily slipping into the realm of fiction by reproducing these conversations.

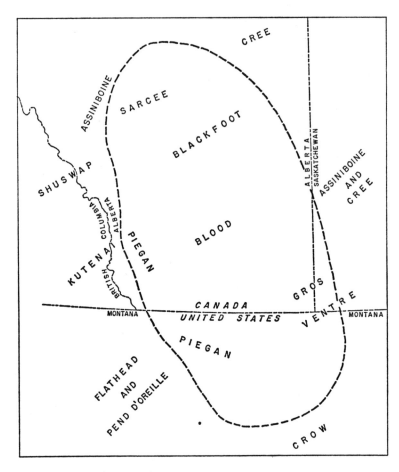

LANDS OF THE BLACKFEET NATION
FROM ABOUT 1800 TO 1840

moccasins. This was Blackfoot Crossing, the heart of the Real People's domain.[6]

Many Names did not stop among the camps of the people here, for these were the southern members of his tribe. The Biters band usually camped farther north, near the edge of the forests and along the Red Deer River.[7] So the family pushed on, along a stream which would one day be named Crowfoot Creek in honor of the small boy now seeing the country for the first time. They passed the Three Hills and continued northward until at last they arrived at the camp of the Biters.

Some time after the family had settled down with the Blackfoot tribe, Shot Close was given a second name. It was not a man's name that had been earned in battle but was another boy's name, a Blackfoot one, given to him by his new father. This name was Bear Ghost, *Kyiah-sta-ah*. Everyone called him that, everyone except his mother, who still loved his first baby name. Even when she was a blind old woman and her son was a great chief, she would grope unseeingly and say, "Shot Close, is that you, my son?"[8]

The first few years in the Blackfoot camp were hard ones for the family, for these were years of sickness and death. In 1836 a terrible epidemic of diphtheria struck the children of the whole Blackfoot nation, killing many infants and youngsters. Bear Ghost and his brother were lucky; they survived.

The next year, 1837, was even worse, for it brought the dreaded smallpox, which had been carried to the northern plains by the American Fur Company's steamer, *St. Peters*. The disease all but wiped out the Mandan tribe, spread to the neighboring Arikaras, and passed northward to the Assini-

---

[6] As late as the turn of the century, it was possible to cross the river in this fashion. However, the ridge has since been washed away.

[7] Interview, March 5, 1957, with Mrs. Jennie Duck Chief, who had lived in Crowfoot's camp and was twenty-six years old when the chief died.

[8] *Ibid.*

boins. At the mouth of the Little Missouri, a Blackfoot Indian was allowed to board the disease-ridden steamer; when he left he became a messenger of death. Although the traders knew they had made a mistake in letting the Indian on board, they did not stop him from leaving.[9]

For two months, no Blackfeet came to trade at Fort McKenzie on the Upper Missouri River. Finally, the chief trader, Alexander Culbertson, went to look for them. After traveling for a few days, he found a camp of about sixty lodges from the Piegan tribe. There was no sound and as he approached, a horrible stench permeated the air. When he came to the first tipi, he saw the grim results of the white man's disease. "Hundreds of decaying forms of human beings, horses and dogs lay scattered everywhere among the lodges," he recorded. "Two old women, too feeble to travel, were the sole living occupants of the village."[10]

During that year, an estimated six thousand Blackfeet, or two-thirds of the whole nation, perished from smallpox. Never again were they quite as numerous as they had been before that tragic year. Somehow, Bear Ghost and the close members of his family escaped the dread disease, but there were few who had not lost loved ones.

By the time the smallpox had run its course, Bear Ghost was eight years old. He had made many friends in his adopted tribe and had begun to reveal his natural abilities for leadership. The old people remembered later that, even when he was a boy, they felt Bear Ghost would become a chief. It did not matter that he had been born a Blood, for Many Names now was his father, and Many Names was a prosperous and respected member of the Blackfoot tribe.

[9] Hiram Martin Chittenden, *The American Fur Trade of the Far West,* II, 619–27.

[10] Bradley, James T., "Affairs at Fort Benton from 1831 to 1869," *Contributions, Historical Society of Montana,* III, 69.

CHAPTER TWO

THE YOUNG WARRIOR

No one knows exactly when Bear Ghost first went to war. He may have been thirteen[1] or he may have been fifteen.[2] Blackfoot tales of war often were embellished with supernatural acts, while the date and place were not considered worthy of recall. For this reason, the telling of Bear Ghost's first and subsequent war exploits can only attempt to follow a logical path through the maze of fact and legend.

When he went on his first raid, Bear Ghost was at the age when boys went out to learn the arts of warfare, usually serving as horse guards or servants to experienced warriors. These trips were part of their education and were an initial step on the path to wealth and glory.

On one of Bear Ghost's early ventures he earned the right to take a man's name. His choice was one from his own family, Packs a Knife, the name of his dead father. Shot Close, Bear Ghost, and Packs a Knife. Each new name in turn replaced the former one. It was a natural progression in a tribe where a man might have as many as eight or ten names during his lifetime. But his new name did not remain with him very long, for there was another name which soon was his. This was *Isapo-muxika*, Crow Indian's Big Foot, or, as interpreters later shortened it, Crowfoot.[3]

[1] Albert Lacombe, "A Great Chieftain," *Macleod Gazette*, May 22 and 29, 1890.

[2] Interview with Drunken Chief by Lucien and Jane Hanks about 1939, from copies of the Hanks's field notes in the author's possession. Also "The Wisdom of Crowfoot" in the Joe Little Chief Papers at the Glenbow-Alberta Institute Archives in Calgary.

[3] This name is taken from three Blackfoot terms, *Isapo* (Crow Indian), *omux* (big), and *okut* (foot).

According to tribal tradition, only one person had previously held this honored name. He was a relative of Many Names, perhaps an uncle or older brother, who had been a victim of treachery two years before young Crowfoot was born. The first Crowfoot had been a brave man whose exploits had made him a chief. One day he and his companions in a war party found a camp which recently had been abandoned by the Crows. Prowling into the clearing, the Blackfeet saw a large footprint in the mud near the edge of a stream. Curiously, each of the other Indians placed his own foot within the imprint, but in each case his foot was too small. Then the chief tried. To the amazement and delight of his comrades, his foot fitted perfectly in the large imprint made by the unknown Crow Indian. Because of this incident, he took the name Crow Indian's Big Foot.

The career of the first Crowfoot ended in disaster in 1828. The Blackfeet agreed to make a peace treaty with the Shoshoni Indians, and Crowfoot headed a delegation of fourteen men to meet their old enemy. But when they crossed the Missouri they were ambushed in the mountains by the Shoshonis, and none of the peace party survived.[4] That dismal year was recorded in the Blackfoot winter counts as "When Crow Indian's Big Foot was killed."[5]

The Blackfeet, quick to avenge such an insult, formed a large war party, which attacked a camp of eight hundred Shoshoni lodges. In the ensuing battle, which lasted a day and a night, the Blackfeet were victorious. Although some story tellers have given young Crowfoot a place in this fight, the winter counts show that he was not yet born. Because of the heroism and treacherous death of the first Crowfoot, he left a name which was highly esteemed. It was felt that such a title

[4] Lacombe, *loc. cit.*
[5] Hugh A. Dempsey, *A Blackfoot Winter Count*, 8.

was worthy only of one who would be a great chief, and for that reason it had remained unused over the many years.

The passing of this name to young Crowfoot is a heroic tale well known to all tribes of the Blackfoot nation. Crowfoot was in his middle teens when the incident occurred. He had been on several war parties and had shown that he was a capable warrior, but he had not yet committed any acts worthy of re-telling around the campfire or in the sacred lodge at the Sun Dance.

As was often the custom, a war party was made up of members of the three tribes, Blackfoot, Blood, and Piegan, under the leadership of a warrior chief of the Blood tribe. They were going on a raid against their old enemies, the Crows. The war party was a big one and included several youths, among whom were Crowfoot and his foster brother, Three Bulls.[6]

The party went south from Blackfoot country, forded the Missouri, and crossed the Judith Basin to the Yellowstone in the present state of Montana. Before reaching that river, the advance scouts returned with a report that a large Crow camp lay ahead. As they drew within sight of the camp, they saw a large lodge painted with four red stripes and recognized it as a Piegan tipi which had been captured by the enemy.

"See that painted lodge?" said the Blood leader. "Whoever gets to it and strikes it will be the future leader of his people in hunting and in war."[7]

On a signal they attacked. Crowfoot ran along a log toward the camp and, as he did so, some Crows who were hiding in the brush opened fire on him. One of the balls struck him in

[6] Three Bulls usually was referred to as Crowfoot's full brother or a maternal half-brother. However, informants indicate that Three Bull's father was Many Names and his mother was Elk in the Water. This would mean that Crowfoot and Three Bulls were not blood relatives. In Blackfoot terminology, however, they would be referred to as brothers.
[7] Interview with Heavy Shield, March 8, 1957.

the arm, passing through his flesh but missing the bone.[8] Crowfoot stumbled and fell but got up again and rushed toward the painted tipi. By this time he was ahead of the others and several Crows were shooting at him, but he reached the striped lodge and struck it with his whip before falling to the ground. Three Bulls, who was close behind him, helped him to the safety of a nearby cutbank.

After the raid was over, the warriors gathered around the wounded boy. When Crowfoot told them that he had struck the tipi, his statement was verified by several who had witnessed the daring act.

"Because of this deed," said the boy, "I will take the name of Crowfoot."

The leader of the party nodded. "Yes," he agreed. "You have struck the tipi and you will become a leader of your people."[9]

Withdrawing triumphantly from enemy territory, the war party retraced its old path until the warriors arrived at a Blood camp. As they approached, Crying Bear, the uncle of Crowfoot, came out to meet them.[10] Following the custom of giving a gift to the first person met on return from a raid, Crowfoot presented his uncle with the design from the tipi which he had struck. Because he had performed the brave deed, Crowfoot was considered to be the owner of the design and could paint it on any tipi which he made. Instead, he gave it to his relative and said, "You can get songs for it and make it holy." This lodge became known as the *omux-sik'sipi-kokah*, or Big Striped Tipi. The design and ceremonies later were given to the All Short People band of Bloods and was last owned by John Cotton, who died in 1957.

During his days as a youth and a young man, Crowfoot

[8] Interview with One Gun, March 5, 1957.
[9] Interview with Joe Crowfoot, March 7, 1957.
[10] Interview with Heavy Shield, as cited.

went on many more raids. In all, he fought in nineteen battles and was wounded six times.[11] He proved to everyone that he could be brave and even merciless in times of war. And as soon as he had a chance, he showed that his was the bravery of a leader, not of a follower. Before he put aside his war knife, he had led several raids and had no trouble recruiting young warriors to accompany him.

As was the custom, Crowfoot had a special comrade who went with him on all his raids. Comrades looked after each other in battle, saw that the other was not left behind, and alternated in their firing so that one always would have a charge in his gun while the other performed the involved task of reloading. Crowfoot and his comrade, Wolf Orphan, went to war together until they were about twenty. One Gun, a grandson of Wolf Orphan, recalled that Crowfoot was a good warrior because he would endure bitter cold and would be the first to swim dangerous rivers. And when they were in enemy country, he often would take a place on a high hill, watching for any suspicious signs.[12]

Although the Blackfeet seldom went to war in winter, Crowfoot made at least one such journey with his foster father. The war party went to steal horses from the Shoshonis, who were camped in the mountains. They made their raid but were discovered, and Crowfoot was shot in the back. Many Names rushed to his side and, with the aid of an old man, got him on a horse and back to safety. There the old man, a shaman, treated and cured him.[13] However, the wound was to plague Crowfoot as he grew older, for the lead ball never was removed.

In other raids Crowfoot was more successful and partici-

[11] Lacombe, *loc. cit.*
[12] Interview with One Gun, as cited.
[13] Interview with Duck Chief by Hanks, about 1939.

pated in some in which herds of fifty to one hundred horses were stolen from the enemy.[14] On one occasion, he was a member of a Blackfoot party which was going on foot to raid the Crees. Some distance north of their own camp they met a Cree party coming south on a similar mission. The Blackfeet opened fire at close range; the Crees fought back, then retreated toward some bushes. Crowfoot was among the first to rush into the fight, where he singled out a Cree warrior who was running toward the trees. To travel more quickly, Crowfoot hurled aside his rifle as he ran after his enemy. The Cree reached the dense bushes, but Crowfoot followed him. Risking ambush, he plunged along the trail until he came close enough to grab the Cree by the hair. Wrenching him backward, Crowfoot plunged a knife into his chest and killed him on the spot. He then hacked the scalp from the Cree's head and returned to his comrades, who had also been victorious. Because of the personal danger he had risked, both by dropping his gun and by following his enemy into the bushes, Crowfoot was praised for his actions. Later, the knife that he had used for the deed was ornamented with feathers and became his prized possession.

On another occasion, Crowfoot led a Blackfoot party which raided the Crees. In the battle, both sides became entrenched in rifle pits. From these defenses, each side showered the other with rifle balls and arrows. Crowfoot, tiring of this kind of fighting, left the safety of his barricade and crawled along the ground toward the enemy lines. Arrows and balls whistled past him, but he kept moving forward until he found a shallow depression midway between the two lines. Then, reaching into his firebag, he withdrew his pipe and turned to his comrades, shouting, "*Oki*, come and smoke with me!"

[14] *Ibid.*

18

His friends saw that this was an invitation to join him in his new position and, if they did not come forward, they would be cowards for refusing to smoke with him. Some of the warriors cautiously began to crawl along the ground; the Crees, seeing them approaching, retreated from their position. Quickly the Blackfeet rushed forward and completely routed them.[15]

The elders also recalled other brave exploits. They told of the time when Crowfoot snatched a loaded rifle from the hands of a Flathead warrior[16] and when he encountered a lone Crow Indian and grabbed his pipe ax but let the warrior go free.[17] Such an instance of mercy was almost unknown to the Blackfeet.

These deeds and the others that made up his nineteen battles gave Crowfoot an enviable reputation as a warrior. All his fights took place during his youth, in the 1840's, when the Blackfoot nation was rich in horses, controlled most of southern Alberta and northern Montana, and carried on an almost incessant war with any tribes which seemed to threaten their domain.

To the north were the Crees, to the east the Assiniboins, to the south the Crows, and across the mountains the Kutenais, Shoshonis, Nez Percés, Flatheads, and Pend d'Oreilles. Other battles were fought from time to time with the Sioux, Ojibwas, and mixed-blood buffalo hunters.

The Blackfeet were in a strategic location, for they could buy guns and other weapons from the British or American traders and maintain large horse herds in their prairie domain. The tribes to the north and east often were well armed but lacked horses, while many of those to the south and west did

[15] Interview with Joe Crowfoot, as cited.
[16] Interview with Buck Running Rabbit by Hanks, about 1939.
[17] Interview with Heavy Shield, as cited.

not have easy access to the valuable trade goods needed for war. So, although surrounded by enemies, the Blackfeet were secure in their own land. Even the white man was not prepared to question their control of the vast prairies.

CHAPTER THREE

LIFE IN THE CAMPS

During the years of his youth and young manhood, Crowfoot's life was not devoted entirely to warfare. He was part of a complex social system filled with societies, ceremonies, and taboos. There were hunting parties, in which buffalo were driven over sheer cliffs and those which were not killed by the fall were shot in bloody corrals below. There were the frequent travels across the prairies in search of food. And there were love, marriage, and children.

As he grew into manhood, Crowfoot became tall and lithe like most of his comrades, but he was thinner and never quite as robust. Besides his relative frailty, he was troubled by a bad leg caused by an enemy ball striking his kneecap.

Even in his youth, Crowfoot was reserved and quiet. Although he had a quick and violent temper, he did not often show it and, when he did, it quickly passed. He seldom joined in social activities and took no part in religious activities. He had about him, even at that early date, a quality which was described as "chiefliness."[1] There was restraint, but without shyness or awkwardness. He was outwardly a follower of the native religion but did not join the secret societies. He attended the rituals with his people and recounted his coups in the main medicine lodge, but throughout his life he had little interest in spiritual matters.

In many ways this was unusual, for the life of a Blackfoot was governed by his religious beliefs. The Sun was the all-powerful spirit, and dreams were the means of gaining in-

[1] Interview with Many Guns by Hanks, about 1939.

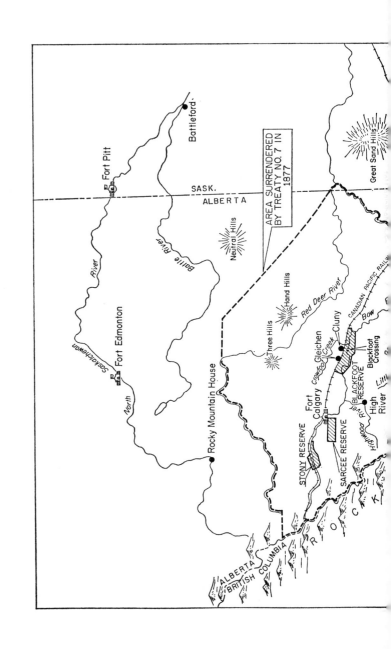

AREA SURRENDERED BY TREATY NO. 7 IN 1877

Great Sand Hills

Battleford·

Fort Pitt

SASK.
ALBERTA

Neutral Hills

Battle River

River

Fort Edmonton

Saskatchewan

North

Rocky Mountain House

Three Hills

Hand Hills

Red Deer River

CANADIAN PACIFIC RAILW

Bow

Cluny

Gleichen

Crowfoot Creek

Blackfoot Crossing

BLACKFOOT RESERVE

Fort Calgary

STONY RESERVE

SARCEE RESERVE

Highwood River

High River

Lit

R   O   C   K

ALBERTA
BRITISH COLUMBIA

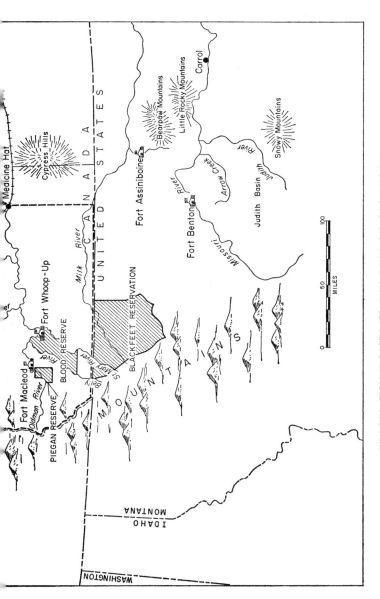

PLACES SIGNIFICANT IN THE LIFE OF CROWFOOT

fluence and power. A man who had holy dreams might become a shaman, a healer, or an adviser to young persons going on the warpath. Many men who became great leaders attributed much of their success to their supernatural influences. Men such as Old Sun, who led the All Medicine Men band, and Calf Shirt of the Bloods, who reputedly received his powers from the grizzly bear, gained ceremonial prestige to enhance their natural abilities of leadership. Crowfoot, in ignoring this aspect of Blackfoot life, neglected an important means of increasing his influence, yet his abilities seemed to far outweigh any loss of prestige from his disinterest in religious life.

In later years, this lack of interest was demonstrated when missionaries wished to bring their Christian doctrine to the Blackfoot nation. While many Blackfeet were opposed to such teachings, Crowfoot welcomed the missionaries to his camp and let them hold services. Such action gained the ill will of the shamans but strengthened Crowfoot's position with the whites. As for Crowfoot himself, while the Sun Dance had no appeal to him, neither did he ever seriously consider converting to Christianity. Although he let the missionaries come to his camp, he had no personal interest in their teachings but merely extended his friendship toward a group of white men whom he felt were trying to help his people.

Another indication of Crowfoot's lack of concern for religious and social conformity was his tipi. The painted lodge was a popular possession of the Blackfeet, particularly those who were rich or important. Connected with it were the sacred songs and rituals bought from the previous owner, obtained through bravery in battle, or given in a holy dream. Throughout his early and middle life, Crowfoot's tipi was plain, without the designs expected of a great man. Only in later years, when he was about fifty years old, did he paint his lodge with a design given him by an adopted son.[2]

Yet, surrounded as he was by supernatural beliefs, Crowfoot did not remain entirely free of their influence. He had in his possession two objects which were his holy protectors—a pair of leggings and an owl's head. The leggings were given to him through a dream when he was a young man; it is the only such dream he was known to have had. In this vision, a buffalo spirit came to him and told him that he would become the "father of his people"—that he would look after the Blackfeet as a father his children. The buffalo spirit instructed Crowfoot to make a pair of leggings from the skin of a buffalo calf and to wear them as his holy charm.

The owl's head was perhaps more important to Crowfoot, in that he wore it constantly until he died. It was given to him by Three Suns, his predecessor as chief. At the time of the gift, Crowfoot was a rising young warrior beginning to reveal many qualities of leadership. When giving him the owl's head, Three Suns told Crowfoot that this would be his protection and if he always carried it he would become a great leader. This object was worn in Crowfoot's hair throughout his life and had holy songs to go with it. At the time of the chief's death, special mourning songs were sung to the head in the hope that it could bring him back to life.

In social activities, Crowfoot joined only one group, the All Brave Dogs, a society of men of his own age.[3] He was fairly active, although not a leader, and on at least one occasion was rebuked by them for supposedly showing poor manners. The tribe had been holding its annual Sun Dance in the Hand Hills, with the Bloods having their ceremonies nearby. During this time, a war party of twelve Pend d'Oreille Indians attacked the Blackfoot camp and killed one of the warriors. The enemy

[2] This adopted son was Poundmaker, who later became a noted chief of the Crees.

[3] Interviews with Mrs. Jennie Duck Chief, March 5, and Joe Crowfoot, March 7, 1957.

then fled toward the Blood camps, where they stopped long enough to kill one man and wound a woman.

The pursuing Blackfeet were led by Big Swan, with Crowfoot and a number of All Brave Dogs forming part of the group. Because of delaying to fight the Bloods, the Pend d'Oreilles were caught, and in the fight that followed ten were killed and two escaped. After the battle, the All Brave Dogs dashed forward to capture the enemies' guns and to count coups on their bodies. In the excitement, a young Blackfoot named Brave Dog grasped a rifle at the same time as Crowfoot, but claimed he had it first. Crowfoot refused to give it up, so Brave Dog let it go and picked up another rifle.

Brave Dog and two of his companions were angry at Crowfoot's refusal to give up the gun and on their return to camp decided to ridicule him. That evening they held a victory dance and invited members of the All Brave Dogs to attend. Crowfoot knew he could not refuse to attend, as every member of the society had to be there or face public criticism. During the evening, Brave Dog arose and called out tauntingly to Crowfoot, "Come and take this gun away from me."[4] Seated among his friends, Crowfoot made no move. People behind him muttered that he should not steal guns from his companions, and others laughed at him for refusing to accept the challenge. Crowfoot was not afraid, but he had been drawn into a situation where further action would have meant trouble for everyone in the camp. If he had accepted Brave Dog's challenge, the young man would have had to try to kill him or face the accusation of being a coward. If a fight had occurred, a feud between opposing families could have torn the camp apart. It was a bitter evening for Crowfoot. Proud and sensitive, he was stung by the public rebuke, particularly when he felt it was unjustified.

[4] Interview with Many Guns by Hanks, as cited.

But even in the face of such an insult, Crowfoot showed why he was capable of leading his people. A few days after the incident he sought out Brave Dog and his friends and praised them for their bravery in publicly rebuking him when they believed they were justified in doing so.

During these years while Crowfoot was growing up, the Blackfeet experienced one of their most stable periods of the century. Their hunting grounds were relatively free of strangers, except for the occasional incursion of mixed-bloods from Red River or from settlements on the Saskatchewan River. The tribe's trade was mostly with the Hudson's Bay Company, either at Fort Edmonton or Rocky Mountain House, with the latter being the most popular post because of its proximity to the plains. To the south, the Bloods and Piegans also traded with the American Fur Company at its posts along the Missouri; sometimes the Blackfeet, too, took their buffalo robes to the southern posts.

But while their hunting grounds still were free of white men, the lands beyond the Blackfeet were rapidly being exploited. The buffalo were being pushed farther and farther west, while visions of fur and gold were bringing many adventurers up the Missouri River.

In the early 1850's, the American government formulated a plan to build a railway across the northern plains to the Pacific Ocean, and in 1853 Congress appropriated $150,000 for field explorations. By this time, treaties had been signed with most of the plains tribes on the American side, except for the Blackfeet, who had been avoided as a hostile and warlike nation. But the need for railroad explorations made a treaty necessary, and in 1854 James Doty was sent out to find the Blackfoot tribes. He traveled as far north as Blackfoot Crossing, seventy miles east of the present city of Calgary, in his search for "American" Indians. After concluding a number of successful meetings, Doty was told of a camp of some one hundred and seventy lodges of Blackfeet on the Red Deer River farther north, but he felt that these were "British" Indians who did not normally live or hunt south of the International Boundary. Among this northern group was the Biters band, with Crowfoot as one of its warriors; none was invited to make peace with the Americans.

In the following year, the Indians visited by Doty were invited to make a formal treaty with the American government, the pact being signed on the Judith River in Montana. Few of the Blackfoot tribe went to the ceremony, and those who did were mostly from the southern part of the territory. Only four signed—Three Bulls, Old Kutenai, The Ridge, and Chief Rabbit Runner—but none was an important chief of the tribe.

The chief of Crowfoot's band at this time was Three Suns, who was one of three prominent leaders of the tribe. The others were Old Sun, head of the All Medicine Men band, and Old Swan, leader of the Bad Guns. These three men were the patriarchs of the tribe and, of them, Old Swan was the most important and respected. For more than half a century he had been a wise counselor to his people and had done much to maintain friendship with the fur traders and with other tribes.

In about 1858, when Crowfoot was twenty-eight, the old chief died and the leadership of the Bad Guns band was taken by a nephew named Big Swan. He was a completely different kind of chief. Where Old Swan had been peaceful, Big Swan was warlike. Where Old Swan had advocated friendship with the whites, Big Swan despised them. He was described by a trader as "a man of colossal size and savage disposition, crafty and treacherous."[5] Although he was a dynamic leader, he was not popular, even with his own people, with the result that many families left his camp to join the band of Three Suns.

[5] William Francis Butler, *The Great Lone Land*, 313.

The Blackfeet used the travois to haul their possessions as well as small children in their nomadic wanderings. Courtesy Smithsonian Institution.

Blackfoot women erecting a tipi in the traditional manner. Courtesy Western History Collections, University of Oklahoma Library.

30

A Blackfoot camp on the prairies.

31

Blackfeet crossing a river, from *Canadian Pictures*, 1881.

Vast herds of buffalo roamed the Blackfoot hunting grounds for more than two-thirds of Crowfoot's life. Courtesy Western History Collections, University of Oklahoma Library.

Father Albert Lacombe attempting to halt a battle between the Blackfeet and Crees. Wounded, his life was saved by Crowfoot. The sketch is by Frederick Remington.

Rocky Mountain House, a Hudson's Bay Company post where the Blackfeet traded, from a sketch attributed to Jean L'Heureux.

34

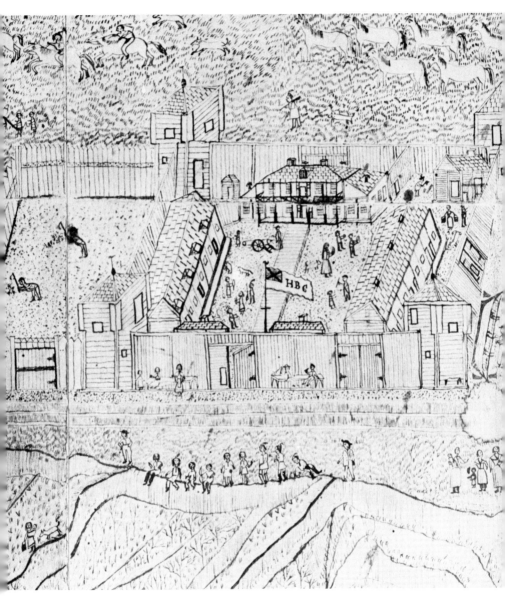

35

Trading room of a Hudson's Bay Company
post. Trade was conducted through an iron
grating.

36

The North West Mounted Police on their great march westward
in 1874. From a contemporary sketch.

C Troop at Fort Macleod, wearing forage caps.

F Troop at Fort Calgary, wearing helmets.

Colonel James F. Macleod of the North
West Mounted Police.

Fort Macleod in about 1876.

Interpreter Jerry Potts served as lia-
ison between Colonel Macleod and
the Blackfeet.

Sioux Chief Sitting Bull, who fled
into Canada in the aftermath of the
Battle of the Little Bighorn.

Crowfoot, in his earliest known picture, an 1875 sketch by Dr. Neavitt of the North West Mounted Police.

Old Sun, Crowfoot's fellow head chief, was too old and feeble by the time the Blackfeet's troubles began to help solve them.

During Crowfoot's thirtieth year, Old Sun died and was succeeded by his son, who bore the same name as his father. This new chief was a leading warrior who also was bitterly opposed to the whites. On one occasion he had killed and scalped a trader on the Missouri River; another time he led a war party in attacking a wagon train of settlers near the Porcupine Hills and slaughtered every man, woman, and child. For years he carried the blond scalp of a young girl whom he had killed during that raid.

Within three years, then, the Blackfoot tribe had lost two of its best leaders, men whose steadying influence had contributed much to maintaining friendly relations with the traders. There is little doubt that the chief factor at Fort Edmonton was worried when the likable Old Swan passed away and was doubly concerned to see a second warrior chief replace another respected elder. He predicted troublesome times ahead for the Hudson's Bay Company. One old chieftain, even an influential man like Three Suns, would have a hard time in restraining the hot-blooded youths.

The factor was right, for shortly after the death of Old Swan the trouble began. In March, 1861, the factor commented in exasperation:

> ... the Blackfeet have been un-bearable for the last 3 years or more, always getting worse and worse destroying our Crops, stealing our Horses and doing everything they could to annoy us, in order to provoke a quarrel so as to kill us. They now threaten openly to kill Whites, Halfbreeds or Crees wherever they find them and to burn Edmonton Fort. . . .[6]

The unrest continued through the early 1860's, culminating in the summer of 1865 with an attack on the outpost of Fort

---

[6] Fort Edmonton journal, 1860–61, entry for March 28, 1861, in Hudson's Bay Company Journals and Correspondence (H.B.C. Arch.B.60/a/31).

Pitt, about one hundred and fifty miles downstream from Fort Edmonton. Bent more on mischief than warfare, the Blackfeet climbed the walls of the fort, stole what was not kept behind locked doors, and destroyed thirteen carts belonging to fort employees.[7]

But this attack was overshadowed by other news from the plains. Three Suns, last of the peaceful chiefs, was dead! The only restraining influence was gone and traders now faced the real danger of having their forts pillaged and destroyed.

By this time, Crowfoot had gained a good reputation in his adopted tribe. The fact that he was a Blood Indian was unimportant, as he took a Blackfoot wife and became a part of Blackfoot society. Many Names was part of a well-to-do family, and as Crowfoot grew up he too became rich; he also was a fine orator and had been a close companion of the late chief. He had made many trips to Fort Edmonton and Rocky Mountain House and had become a good friend of the chief trader, Richard Hardisty. The trader in turn had encouraged Crowfoot, after noticing his keen intelligence and his friendly disposition toward the whites.

Crowfoot, like other leaders of that period, did not fully understand the white men, but he believed they had their own supernatural powers. Some Indians thought this power lay in the strange pieces of paper upon which the traders could make magic marks for other white men to read. Some thought that their fair skin made them relatives of *Napi*, the mythical Blackfoot deity who was said to have had white skin and a long beard. While Crowfoot may have shared some of these beliefs, he also was wise enough to see white men simply as men, some good and some bad. He knew their trade goods were beneficial to his people, and the buffalo hides, horses, and dried meat

---

[7] William J. Christie, Carlton House, to James R. Clare, Fort Garry, September 2, 1865, *ibid.* (H.B.C. Arch.B.60/b/2, fo.254).

they wanted in exchange were plentiful in his land. As long as white men, as individuals, extended a hand of friendship to him, he treated them like any other men.

This was the guiding philosophy of his life. If the person was helpful to his people, he was a friend. If he was a threat, he was an enemy. It did not matter whether he was white, half-blood, or Indian.

After Three Suns's death, the chance of being chosen successor seemed most favorable for the old chief's son, a young man who had taken his father's name. The younger Three Suns (also called The Sun and White Little Dog) was well liked and had a good war record but lacked the decisive qualities of his father. Crowfoot also was a candidate, but, as far as some of the Blackfeet were concerned, he was not related to Three Suns and was not eligible. Although leadership was not hereditary, a son or nephew usually was favored to fill such a vacancy.

In the weeks that followed, more and more members of the band began to favor Crowfoot, while relatives of the old chief remained firmly with Three Suns. For a time there were fears that an argument might arise, but at last the camp split into two groups, with about twenty-seven lodges going with Three Suns and twenty-one with Crowfoot.[8] The people continued to travel together and camp near each other, but they were in the first stages of forming two separate bands. Three Suns's group retained the name of the Biters, while Crowfoot's following eventually became known as the Big Pipes.[9]

As the autumn of 1865 passed, the bands wandered north to their winter camping grounds at the edge of the bushlands.

[8] Alfred Sully to E. S. Parker, commissioner of Indian affairs, Washington, D.C., July 16, 1870, enclosing census of the Blackfoot nation, in the National Archives, Washington, D.C.

[9] In later years this band became known as the Moccasins, or *Tsikin-aiee*.

The northern part of the tribe straggled out along the banks of the Battle River and, although uncomfortably close to the Crees, they planned to pass a quiet winter in a good buffalo-hunting area. Crowfoot, although not yet a real chief, led his followers a few miles downstream from Three Suns's camp. Farther along the river were two larger camps of more than a hundred lodges which made up the rest of the tribe.

At the same time, a large camp of Crees, Assiniboins, and Ojibwas, all enemies of the Blackfeet, were encamped about fifty miles to the northeast. And the Cree scouts knew exactly where the Blackfeet were camped.

CHAPTER FOUR

CROWFOOT BECOMES A CHIEF

Late in 1865, Crowfoot first met Albert Lacombe, a man who was to figure prominently in spreading the Blackfoot leader's reputation throughout the world. Lacombe was an Oblate priest who had been in the West for thirteen years and had just been assigned the mission of "coursing the prairies to try and reach the poor savage Crees and Blackfeet."[1]

Leaving his mission headquarters at St. Albert in October, Lacombe had gone to a Piegan camp on the Red Deer River, where he had stayed, "giving instructions, baptizing the children and visiting the sick."[2] From there he had traveled north to the Battle River, and on December 3 he reached the camp of Crowfoot. Here the priest met the Blackfoot leader and learned that his camp and Three Suns's soon would be uniting for mutual protection for the winter. After a night in Crowfoot's camp, Lacombe went upstream to Three Suns's village, where he planned to stay until the two bands were united.

That night the air was shattered by the sounds of gunshots

[1] Katherine Hughes, *Father Lacombe, the Black-Robe Voyageur*, 105. Albert Lacombe was born at St. Sulpice, Quebec, on February 27, 1827, his great-grandfather being a Saulteaux Indian. He was ordained in 1849 and came west as a missionary in 1852. During his years on the prairies he was known and respected by the Indians, whites, and mixed-bloods of every denomination. He founded the village of St. Albert, Alberta, in 1861, wrote dictionaries and grammars on Indian languages, and pioneered much of the work of the Order of Mary Immaculate in Alberta. He founded the Lacombe Home near Calgary in 1909 and died there on December 12, 1916.

[2] Father Lacombe to the superior general, Mission of St. Albert, January 6, 1866: "I have just passed two days among them, to give them some instructions, baptize their children and visit their sick. . . ." (*Missions de la Congregation des Missionaires Oblats de Marie Immaculée*, 234.)

49

and the terrible cry of an attacking enemy. Instantly Three Suns grabbed his musket and shouted a warning to his warriors, "*Assinow! Assinow!* The Crees! The Crees!" Enemy warriors, then about a hundred yards away, poured a fusillade on the unguarded camp. As the priest told it:

> In an instant some score of bullets came crashing through the leather lodge and the wild war whoop of the Crees broke forth through the sharp and rapid detonation of many muskets. . . . the groans of the dying, the yelling of the warriors, the harangues of the chiefs, and the noise of dogs and horses, all mingled, formed a kind of hell.[3]

The Blackfeet, eighty warriors with only sixty muskets among them, were hopelessly outnumbered by the well-armed enemy party of more than eight hundred men.[4] Once the raiders almost overran the camp, but, urged on by Three Suns, his warriors fought back and pushed them to the edge of the camp. While some Crees were attacking and retreating, others were searching among the lodges for dead and wounded victims to scalp.

Three times during the long night the Crees surged into the camp, but each time they were repulsed. The dead and the dying lay among the littered debris, and each time a renewed attack was made, more bodies crumpled to the ground. To add to the confusion, a steady snow fell, casting an eerie pallor over the battlefield.

During the night, Father Lacombe tried to contact the Crees and stop the battle, but his voice and familiar black-robed figure went unnoticed in the darkness, so he spent the night caring for the wounded and offering prayers for the dying.

In the early morning, when the first pale light was casting

---

[3] Lacombe, "A Great Chieftain," *loc. cit.*
[4] Hughes, *Father Lacombe*, 121.

gray shadows over the snow-laden sky, the priest made another attempt to stop the fight. Grasping his white flag emblazoned with a red cross, he crawled to a small elevation in view of the enemy lines. The Blackfeet, seeing him go, halted their fire as the priest arose and began waving his banner. He called to the Crees in their own tongue and begged them to stop the senseless fight, but his voice was unheeded and the morning still was too dark to reveal his tiny flag. The shooting continued and a bullet ricocheted from a stone, struck the priest on the shoulder, and grazed his forehead. When Father Lacombe crumpled to the ground, two warriors rushed to his side and carried him to the Blackfoot camp. There they discovered that the bullet which had struck him had been almost spent and had done little more than break the skin.

In the early morning, when the snow stopped and the air cleared, the sound of battle was heard downriver at Crowfoot's camp. Quickly the leader gathered his warriors and sent messengers to other camps in the area. At about ten o'clock on the morning of December 5, his men burst upon the besieged camp. Screaming their war cries, the Blackfoot warriors led by Crowfoot raced through the camp and struck the enemy in a withering onslaught. By this time the Crees had taken almost half the camp, but they fell back to a nearby hill in the face of the new attackers.

Although still outnumbering their foes, the Crees became disorganized; the chiefs, seeing that a disastrous rout might occur, told their men to withdraw. Reinforced with about three hundred captured Blackfoot horses and the trophies and scalps from the pillaged camp, they gradually retreated north until they reached the safety of the bushlands.

Crowfoot had brought great honor to his name that morning. He had fought like a bear, completely ignoring any danger to himself, and had led his warriors in an attack that had caused the larger enemy force to retreat. His timely rescue had saved the camp, while the presence of the priest, who had previously labored almost exclusively among the Crees, was a great moral victory for the tribe.

Returning to the camp after the battle, Crowfoot found it in shambles. Twelve men, women, and children had been killed, fifteen wounded, two children kidnaped, and the whole horse herd stolen. The supply of dried meat and pemmican had been taken, and almost half of the lodges were so badly damaged they were unusable. Many months later he learned that, besides the eight Cree bodies found at the scene, the enemy had carried away another twelve to prevent their mutilation.[5]

Stopping at the tattered remains of the chief's lodge, Crowfoot found that Three Suns and the priest both were injured. Three Suns's leg had been shattered by an enemy bullet, while Father Lacombe still was weak from the glancing blow.

In later years, this incident was to be the most colorful episode of the priest's adventurous life. On his many trips to eastern Canada, the United States, and Europe during fundraising expeditions for his missions, the story of the attack and Crowfoot's dramatic rescue served as a classic example of life among the savage Indians. But, in his first report of the affray,[6] Father Lacombe had no idea that the man who saved his life would someday be a famous chief. So, when relating the incident, he made no direct mention of Crowfoot. Only in later years did he stress the chief's prominent part in turning the tide of battle. In doing this, he helped promote the fame of Crowfoot and at the same time gave added prestige to his own cause.

In the spring of 1866, the tribe again split into small bands

[5] Father Émile Legal to James Pilling, Washington, D.C., September 20, 1889, from copy in possession of the author.
[6] *Missions*, 224–62.

and drifted out on the prairies in search of buffalo. After the spring hunt they congregated for the annual Sun Dance, at which Crowfoot performed another deed which surpassed even his acts in the great winter battle.

Some women had gone to collect berries for the religious ceremonies and had taken a young boy along to guard them. They found a good patch of saskatoons and were busily picking when a huge grizzly bear crashed through the bushes toward them. Screaming, the women dropped their bags and rushed for the camp. The youth, remembering his duty, tried to fit an arrow into his bow, but the grizzly smashed it from his hand and tore at his flesh.

When those at the camp learned what had happened, the All Brave Dogs galloped up to the grove of trees. With Crowfoot among the leaders they shouted and fired shots to frighten the bear away from the boy, who was badly mauled but still alive. The warriors wanted to kill the bear immediately, but Crowfoot stopped them and instructed them to ride to the other side of a grove of trees in which the animal was hiding. Once there, they were to induce the bear to attack them and to let him know when it had been lured into sight.

While the whole camp gathered at a safe distance, the All Brave Dogs rode to the other side of the grove. There, single riders went into the trees and tried to entice the grizzly toward them. When at last the huge beast came into view, the men shouted to Crowfoot, who was waiting on the far side. Quickly he guided his horse into the dense bushes and soon was behind the savage bear. With deadly accuracy he plunged a spear into the animal and, when his horse became too frightened, dismounted and continued to stab the bear until its lifeless body crashed to the ground.[7]

This incident of bravery made such a profound impression

[7] Lacombe, *loc. cit.*, and interview with Joe Crowfoot, March 7, 1957.

53

on the Blackfeet that much of its success was attributed to supernatural power. People pointed out that even the spear Crowfoot used was a special one made from the knife used to kill a Cree several years before. But they also recognized Crowfoot's fearlessness, and from that time on he was recognized throughout the tribe as a prominent chief.

When word reached Fort Edmonton and Rocky Mountain House about Crowfoot's leadership, the traders were pleased, for in him they believed they had a good friend. And at this time they needed all the friends they could get, for during 1866 relations continued to be uneasy between the Hudson's Bay Company people and the Blackfeet. To add to the problem, the Bloods and Piegans had become involved in a number of disputes with white settlers along the Missouri River. The Bloods had wiped out the budding town of Ophir the year before in retaliation for the murder of one of their chiefs. Then, during the winter, four Piegans were killed in a clash with whites, and the tribe responded by attacking a mission farm on Sun River. By spring, Montana settlers were convinced that they had a Blackfoot war on their hands, while many young warriors were anxious to make the war a reality. For the next four years, there were sporadic raids upon the Montana frontier; the United States Army established Fort Cooke and Fort Shaw for the protection of the settlers.

In the autumn of 1866, some of the Bloods and Piegans who usually traded on the Missouri decided to go north to avoid further conflict with the Americans. Reaching the Red Deer River country, they met the main camp of Sarcees and received the news that a large portion of the Cree tribe was camped near Fort Edmonton.

Seen From Afar, head chief of the Bloods, announced that they would turn back, but before doing so he would send a messenger to Fort Edmonton, asking for a trading party to be dispatched to his camp. In response to this request, an expedition of fifteen mixed-blood traders and thirty Red River carts was sent out under the direction of John Cunningham. When they arrived at the camp near the end of October most of the Blackfeet, all of the Sarcees, and large numbers of Bloods and Piegans were there.

As soon as they entered the camp, Cunningham had a feeling there would be trouble. Many of the Blackfeet stood sullenly, watching the creaking carts and Cree mixed-blood drivers go by. The warriors who had attacked Fort Pitt the previous summer arrogantly displayed themselves and made no attempt to hide the horses which bore the brands of white traders and settlers.

Cunningham stopped in front of Seen From Afar's lodge and drew the carts into a protective circle. The Blood chief's pipe was taken from its sacred place at the back of the lodge and was circulated among the chiefs and traders as a symbol of friendship. Cunningham noticed that the only chiefs who smoked were the Bloods, Piegans, some of the Sarcees, and Crowfoot from the Blackfeet.

The trading began quietly enough, with the Bloods and Piegans offering horses, pemmican, and buffalo robes in exchange for ammunition, paint, blankets, tobacco, and other goods. The traders had obtained about twenty-five horses and a good supply of meat from the southern tribes when Cunningham heard a commotion at the edge of the camp. Looking beyond the crowd of customers, he saw Big Eagle, a warrior, and Big Swan, the hulking Blackfoot chief, waving their guns and haranguing a party of warriors who were gathered around them. Then, turning toward the carts, Big Swan pushed his way through the crowd and gave a long speech attacking the traders and the Cree mixed-bloods in the party.

Realizing that any further trading would be impossible,

Cunningham began to repack the carts but was stopped by Big Swan, who claimed he had buffalo robes to barter. When the chief dropped two or three of them at the trader's feet, Cunningham picked one up, examined it, and dropped it in disgust. They were dirty, worn hides which had no value and were presented only to insult the trader. When Cunningham refused to trade, the chief pushed him aside and led his warriors to pillage the carts of their trade goods. When the carts were empty, Big Swan waved his gun threateningly at the mixed-bloods, but at this point Seen From Afar stepped between them. The traders were there at his invitation and he would not let them be harmed.

As the Blood chief stood alone in the clearing, Big Swan quivered with rage and urged his men to ignore him and to kill the traders. But as he spoke, Crowfoot stepped from the crowd and joined Seen From Afar at the carts. Turning savagely to Big Swan, he spat, "You people are dogs! The whites should sweep you off the face of the earth."[8]

Taken aback by such an outburst from one of his own tribesmen, Big Swan was silenced momentarily. Some other chiefs, encouraged by Crowfoot's action, joined him in the clearing and formed a protective barrier between Big Swan's warriors and the traders. They all were Bloods and Piegans; Crowfoot was the only Blackfoot chief to defy Big Swan.

Taking advantage of the situation, Cunningham formed his caravan and, with an escort provided by Crowfoot and Seen From Afar, he took his empty carts back to Fort Edmonton. The chief factor reported:

Mr. Cunningham gave it as his opinion, that not one of them would have been spared. "Spoke Master General"[9] did all he

8 William J. Christie, Edmonton House, to Richard Hardisty, Rocky Mountain House, November 2, 1866, in Hudson's Bay Company Journals and Correspondence (H.B.C. Arch.B.60/b/2, fos. 595–96, 597, 598).

could to incite the Blackfeet to kill them, "Big Swan" was the next worst, "Natoose" [Three Suns] did nothing, the Circees [Sarcees] looked on and said nothing, but afterwards said the Blackfeet were Dogs. There was only one Blackfoot who spoke like a man, and if ever I see him, I will give him a present, "Is.poo.mux.e.ca" [Crowfoot], a friend of yours. . . .[10]

In defying Big Swan and his warriors, Crowfoot had faced possible death, but no resentment was borne against him. Perhaps some of the warriors privately were relieved that a massacre had not taken place and trade relations severed with the British company. And everyone, even Big Swan, had to admire Crowfoot for the courageous stand he had taken. This was his first decisive action since becoming a chief, and it set a pattern which was to be repeated many times. Crowfoot expected justice from the whites and demanded it from his own people; he was willing to risk his life for it.

This incident, as well as Crowfoot's general attitude toward the whites, made him a welcome visitor at their trading posts. He was presented with a British flag, a chief's uniform of scarlet cloth, and other presents. Regardless of his actual position in the tribe, he was received as though he were a head chief, in the same manner as Old Sun, Three Suns, and Big Swan.

A visit to a trading fort always was an important occasion for the tribe. Not only did the people get new guns and clothing, but there also were kegs of Hudson's Bay rum, which were a stock in trade. For many of the warriors, the trip was a drunken orgy. Crowfoot also was fond of liquor and got drunk on occasion but, as in his everyday life, he was generally a moderate man.

On one occasion when Crowfoot and a number of other

[9] I.e., the orator of the tribe. This refers to Big Eagle, or *Omuxi-peta*.
[10] Christie to Hardisty, *loc. cit.*

Blackfeet were going to Rocky Mountain House to trade, they met a camp of Bloods and North Piegans under the leadership of Rainy Chief and Morning Plume. The tribes combined for mutual protection and sent two messengers ahead to tell the factor they were coming. The two men reached the fort a day ahead of the camp and received a present of tobacco. Five Stony Indians trading at the post were herded inside to prevent trouble and were kept there for several days. The factor was afraid to send them away because their presence might have been known to the messengers, who would inform the others and pursue and kill them.

On the following morning the main camp arrived. Hundreds of lodges were pitched across the river from the fort and the Indians crossed over in a body. Rainy Chief, as the senior chief in the group, led a white horse as a gift for the factor. As he walked forward and shook hands with the traders, the employees inside the stockade fired a volley of shots in salute.

Although there were several minor chiefs in the party, the traders recognized only one man from each tribe: Rainy Chief from the Bloods, Morning Plume from the North Piegans, and Crowfoot from the Blackfeet. Each one was greeted in turn by the factor, and Crowfoot was asked to supply four All Brave Dog guards for the duration of their stay. This was a great honor, as the All Brave Dogs would be under his jurisdiction and would take orders from no one else during the trading expedition. It was their duty to see that no Indians caused trouble with the traders or tried to attack the fort. Night and day they were expected to circle the fort, armed with war clubs. None of them was permitted to drink liquor during the visit but would be given generous gifts on their departure for the plains.

Crowfoot and the two other chiefs were invited into the fort and the gates were locked behind them. While their tribesmen waited on the outside, the trio was greeted warmly by fort employees and given presents. Each received a length of rope tobacco, a bag of leaf tobacco, and a derbylike hat decorated with eagle plumes. Although they were treated as guests, Crowfoot and the other chiefs knew they really were voluntary hostages who would remain inside the fort until the trading was finished. This was their guarantee that no Indians would attack the fort while the trading was under way.

During the entire three days of trading, none of the employees ventured outside the fort, and, if the Blackfeet knew the enemy Stonies were inside, they made no hostile move. When the trading was over, Crowfoot presented the factor with one of his best horses before leading his people back to the plains. Recognition by the traders had added materially to the prestige which he already was gaining through his abilities as a warrior, leader, and spokesman.[11]

From that time on, Crowfoot's reputation continued to grow. Careful management of his horse herd had made him a wealthy man; he was generous and took a sincere interest in the problems of his band. His leadership within his own group was undisputed.

Late in 1869, the dreaded smallpox returned to the Blackfeet. This was the same disease that had wiped out two-thirds of the nation when Crowfoot was a boy, and it was transmitted to the tribes in almost the same way. Some travelers on a Missouri River steamboat had contracted the disease and were confined to a cabin. Attempts were made to isolate them, but these were thwarted in early September when the boat reached the mouth of Milk River in Piegan country. As reported in a Montana newspaper, a Piegan crept aboard

to purloin a blanket from the couch of one of the small pox

[11] Interview with Campbell Munroe, who lived at the fort in the 1860's and 1870's. Copy from Oblate Archives, Edmonton, in author's possession.

patients, while the steamboat discharged its freight at the mouth of that turbid stream. . . . The dreaded disease broke out among the copper-colored devils, and spreading like wildfire from tepee to tepee and from camp to camp, has made a great havoc in their strength and numbers—sending them to perdition in quicker time than bullets and bad bread could do the work.[12]

From the Piegans the disease spread to the neighboring tribes, and one of the first men to die was the great Blood chief Seen From Afar. He soon was followed by hundreds of other men, women, and children from all tribes. Throughout the winter, lodge after lodge was abandoned and the bands were constantly on the move as though pursued by some fearsome specter. Whole families were struck down, until only the camp dogs were left to gnaw on their bones. Handsome young men in the early stages of the disease committed suicide rather than face disfigurement. Everywhere there was pestilence and panic. The forts at Edmonton, Rocky Mountain House, and Pitt closed their doors and refused to trade, while Crees and mixed-bloods were warned to keep away from the Blackfoot camps.

By spring, when the disease had run its course among the Blackfoot tribes, the Indians began to count their losses. The Piegans, who were most severely affected, counted more than a thousand dead, the Bloods and Blackfeet over six hundred each, and the tiny tribe of fifty Sarcee lodges was reduced to only twelve.[13]

Crowfoot, as in the earlier epidemic, escaped the disease, but almost a quarter of his camp was wiped out. And, in the neighboring Biters camp, Three Suns was a victim of the epidemic. Crowfoot, almost as a natural consequence, became

[12] *New North West* (Deer Lodge, Mont.), October 29, 1869.
[13] *The Weekly Manitoban* (Fort Garry), September 16, 1871.

the leader of both bands and assumed the undisputed position of one of the three tribal head chiefs, in company with Old Sun and Big Swan.

After the plague, the Blackfeet began to rebuild their lives. But it never was quite the same, for the epidemic had taken many of their best chiefs and warriors. Never again were they to be quite so arrogant and troublesome to Hudson's Bay traders nor to cast so much terror over such a large territory. The Blackfeet needed time to readjust and grow, but, before they could do so, white man's civilization was upon them.

CHAPTER FIVE

FATHER OF HIS PEOPLE

One day Crowfoot was resting in his lodge when he heard a commotion outside. Going to the doorway, he saw that a strange dog had wandered into camp and was being attacked by his wives' pack dogs.

"*Nitakit!*" he called to his wives. "Stop them! Stop them!" Then, with the help of his women, his own dogs were chased away.

"Here, little one," coaxed Crowfoot, as the strange dog huddled fearfully by the edge of the lodge. "Come here." He told his wives to bring some meat. Stroking the animal, he fed it piece by piece until it was full. Afterward he led it to the edge of the camp and sent it on its way.[1]

To the Blackfeet the incident was symbolical of Crowfoot's leadership. The poorest and most unfortunate creature was welcome in his lodge, whether a frightened dog, a destitute Blackfoot, or a wandering stranger.

While still a young man, Crowfoot had married a Blackfoot girl named Cutting Woman, or *Sisoyaki*, and within the next few years he had taken two more wives, Cloth Woman, *Nipis-tai-aki*, and Packs on her Back, *Ayis-tsi*. The more wives a man possessed, the greater was his wealth, for women could tan hides, make clothing, prepare pemmican, and perform other household chores. At the same time, a man needed to be rich to support more than one or two wives, as each additional

---

[1] This story was told by Joe Crowfoot, grandson of the chief, in an interview, March 7, 1957.

person meant more horses to carry the belongings and more food to be secured.

During his life, Crowfoot had a total of ten wives, although there were seldom more than three or four in his household at a time. Among the others were Prairie Woman, *Sowki-pi-aki*; Killed the Enemy with His Own Gun, *Awatoht-sinik*; Going Out to Meet the Victors, *Pi-ot-skini*; and Paper Woman, *Asinaki*.[2] The latter was a sister of Red Crow, head chief of the Bloods. Of all the wives, Cutting Woman always was first in importance and Crowfoot's favorite. She sat beside him in his lodge and accompanied him on his visits to other tribes.

To keep his large family of wives and relatives, Crowfoot had two tipis. His own was a thirty-buffalo tipi, a type of dwelling which could be used only by the most wealthy men with the best war records. Where the average lodge was made from about twelve buffalo hides, this one was made from thirty skins. It was so large and heavy that it was made in two sections, each being a full load for a horse travois when moving camp. It had two entrances and two campfires, one of which was reserved solely for lighting pipes or burning incense. It was indeed the home of a wealthy man.

In this lodge lived Crowfoot, his wives, his old mother, and his children. Although he had a large number of wives, he had relatively few children, and only four of these reached maturity, a boy and three girls. Most of the others were sickly and died of tuberculosis while still young.[3]

In the second lodge Crowfoot kept his relatives and hired

[2] Interviews with Mrs. Jennie Duck Chief, March 5, and Joe Crowfoot, March 7, 1957.
[3] The son, who had his father's young name of Bear Ghost (shown on the annuity lists as Without Design a Bear), was blind. The daughters were Charged Ahead, Little Woman, and First Beaver. Little Woman outlived all the others by many years and died in the early 1940's.

men. These included his young brother Iron Shield, who had been married but now was a widower; Big Fish, a half-brother; and hired men Wolf Straight Hair, High Eagle, Big Road, Weasel Head, and others. It was the duty of Crowfoot's wives to cook for these men and to carry their water and firewood.[4] In exchange for these services, the young men hunted, guarded the horse herds, and did other work around the camp. Crowfoot was the only chief in the tribe wealthy enough to employ people in this manner.

Each morning the men would come before the chief to receive their instructions. Standing respectfully in front of him, each would be assigned a task which would keep him busy for the day. If the buffalo were near, the men might be told to take the best running horses from the herd and get meat for the camp. Out to the plains they would go, taking extra pack horses to bring back the products of the hunt. The buffalo were killed and butchered on the prairies and the meat carried directly back to the chief's lodge. There Crowfoot directed its disposal to his wives and the needy in his camp. Crowfoot himself never went hunting after he became rich. He always was an indifferent hunter, so with a retinue of skilled men around him he found it unnecessary to join in the hunts.

Each day men also were assigned as horse guards, for either the day or night shift. Crowfoot was the only chief to hire men as twenty-four-hour guards and, as a result, he seldom had any horses stolen or stampeded. In the 1870's, Crowfoot owned about four hundred horses, ranging from the valuable buffalo runners and race horses to common riding and travois ponies. He divided the herd into four groups of a hundred each and grazed them at different locations. This not only eased

---

[4] Details of life in Crowfoot's camp were provided largely by Drunken Chief, son of Iron Shield, who had lived with the chief as a boy, in interview by Hanks, about 1939.

the grass problem but minimized the danger of stampeding in case of a thunderstorm or enemy attack. It was the duty of his guards to stay awake, for a sleeping guard could lose not only the horses but his own life as well. It was not uncommon for drowsy guards to be killed and scalped by enemy war parties before the horse herd was run off. Crowfoot was particular about this point and was enraged if he ever discovered that his men were not properly performing their duties.

Crowfoot also would send his young men through the camp to help the poor. Presents of meat and tobacco would be distributed and horses provided when moving camp. The old people in particular received Crowfoot's constant attention and never had to beg for food or seek transportation whenever he was in a position to help them. This is why they called him *manistokos*, the father of his people, for he looked after his followers as a father cares for his own children.

In the autumn, when the leaves were starting to turn, Crowfoot would lead his people from the prairies to the bush-dotted parkland north of the Red Deer River. Each year he chose a different location for his winter camp, to lessen the danger of an enemy attack. Usually the tribe gathered into about eight small camps, with the farthest ones being about four days' travel apart. Once they were settled, the women worked quickly to gather enough wood before the coming of the heavy snows. When the cold weather came, the Blackfeet did little traveling. Only when the buffalo herds were close by or there was any visiting to be done would they venture far from their camps. They usually did not take to the warpath in winter, although small groups sometimes would take advantage of blizzardy weather to steal horses from the Crees.

In the winter, Crowfoot seldom went visiting. Often other chiefs or friends would come to his lodge and would be welcomed, but it was unusual for Crowfoot to return these visits.

65

He was reserved by nature and preferred the quietness and comfort of his own lodge and the company of his close relatives.

In the spring, when the warm winds melted the snow and the coulees were choked with muddy water, the Blackfeet struck camp and moved out to the plains. The discards and wastes of winter were left behind as the horses and travois formed a long procession from the river bottom out to the treeless prairies. South across the Red Deer and into the Three Hills and Hand Hills country they traveled, watching for the main buffalo herds. These great beasts, with their shaggy winter coats falling out in hairy chunks, wandered over the countryside grazing on the new prairie grass which carpeted the earth. Lumbering and dull-witted, they were easy targets for the steel-tipped arrows of the Blackfoot hunters.

By late spring or early summer, the bands usually had circled around their hunting grounds and had begun to gather at a prearranged location for their annual Sun Dance. This was the ceremony where a pure woman fulfilled a vow made during the year that she would dedicate a Sun Dance if the holy spirit would hear her prayers. It may have been a prayer for the return of a loved one who was on a dangerous mission or to see her husband recover from a terrible sickness. But, whatever the vow, it meant that the woman would offer her thanks in a sacred ceremony in which the whole tribe would participate. It also was the time for warriors to publicly recount their war exploits, the time for men's and women's societies to hold their dances and ceremonies, and for the young men to fulfill their vows by submitting to a self-torture ritual.

When he arrived at the Sun Dance, Crowfoot led his band to its appointed place in the camp, on the east side of the huge circle of tipis. By this time his following was known as the Moccasin band. The whole northern half of the circle consisted of bands which were controlled by minor chiefs but who recognized Crowfoot as their head chief. Westward in the circle from Crowfoot's Moccasin band were the Big Provision Bags under The Eagle and Weasel Calf, the Biters under Running Rabbit, the Many Children under Eagle Calf, the Slapped Faces under White Eagle, and the Skunks under Eagle Ribs.

The southern half of the circle consisted of bands controlled by the other two head chiefs. Immediately south of Crowfoot's camp was the warlike band of Bad Guns under Big Swan, followed by the Liars under Bull Elk, the Strong Ropes under Lone Chief, and the All Medicine Men under Old Sun.[5]

During the Sun Dance, Crowfoot seldom took an active part in the ceremonies, although he did attend them. When the rituals were over, the bands again drifted onto the plains in search of buffalo. In late summer a visit was made to the trading posts, and as autumn came upon them they moved back to their winter camping grounds.

During these nomadic years, Crowfoot was essentially a peaceful man. He had given up the warpath when he was twenty, although his fellow chiefs, Big Swan and Old Sun, still went out against their enemies. Whenever treaties were made with the Crees or other tribes, Crowfoot kept his young men from going on raids, but when they were at war he did not object to their frequent raids into enemy territory. At times he showed leniency when small enemy war parties were discovered, but more often he was merciless in the protection of his camp. And when horses were stolen from his people, he often asked his own young men to join in the pursuit. Because of his bad leg, Crowfoot himself was unable to keep up the steady pace required by such a party.

Every man has faults, and Crowfoot's was his temper. Although normally he was a quiet man, he could flare up sud-

5 Interview with Heavy Shield, March 8, 1957.

denly, particularly if someone disobeyed his orders or questioned his actions. When he thought he was right, he did not want to answer to anyone; it was part of the pride and arrogance which went with his leadership. His was the kind of temper which was quickly ignited and when it was gone he bore no grudges.

This uncontrollable temper was responsible for several incidents, including the stabbing of two fellow chiefs and the threatening of another. The two chiefs, Eagle Calf and Lone Chief, had argued with Crowfoot on separate occasions and, when tempers flared, the head chief had slashed out angrily with his knife. In both cases, Crowfoot and the chiefs had been drinking, and one of the chiefs had a temperament similar to that of his head chief. Neither man was seriously injured and their friendships with Crowfoot were not affected.[6]

A third and more serious incident occurred between Crowfoot and his fellow head chief Old Sun while the Sun Dance was in progress. For reasons known only to himself, Old Sun had decided to leave during the ceremonies and to take his band northward. He had previously agreed to go with Crowfoot's band after the Sun Dance was over, but gave no explanation for changing his mind.

Crowfoot, angered by the announcement, stormed over to Old Sun's camp and found that the elder chieftain already had packed his belongings. Old Sun's wife was leading the first horse travois from the grounds when Crowfoot stopped her. Old Sun came over and, when Crowfoot repeated the request to remain until the end of the ceremony, the older man refused. Angrily Crowfoot exclaimed that it was Old Sun's duty to stay and pointed his rifle at the lead travois horse. But just as he pulled the trigger, someone pushed his arm and the bullet struck the wooden travois frame. Crowfoot glared angrily at

[6] Interview with Duck Chief by Hanks, about 1939.

his fellow chief for a moment, then turned and stalked away.
A short time later, when his temper had cooled, Crowfoot sought out Old Sun and apologized for his conduct. The two had been close companions for several years and the elder man extended his hand in renewed friendship.[7]

Crowfoot may have had other faults, but his temper was the worst. On many occasions it caused embarrassment and strained relations, but the chief never was able to change. Until his dying day he expected to be heard and obeyed.

[7] Interview with Many Guns by Hanks, about 1939.

CHAPTER SIX

A SON LOST AND GAINED

In 1872, two years after the end of the great smallpox epidemic, Big Swan died of tuberculosis. This man had been a fighter until the end. In 1869 he had killed a head chief of the Crees, *Maskepatoon*, during a peacemaking visit and, until the outbreak of the epidemic, he had led his warriors on numerous raids against the Crees, mixed-bloods, and white traders. Low Horn, a relative of the deceased chief, took over the Bad Guns band but did not attain the status of a head chief. This left only two head chiefs in the Blackfoot tribe, Old Sun with a following of about eight hundred persons and Crowfoot with thirteen hundred. Crowfoot was the diplomat and peacemaker, while Old Sun was the warrior and medicine man.

In the autumn of 1873, while Crowfoot was camped in the Three Hills area, one of his sons announced that he was going to war. At that time Crowfoot had three growing sons, but one was dumb and the other's eyes showed signs of early blindness. Only the eldest gave promise of becoming a great warrior. He was much like his father had been in his early teens, tall, lean, and with a deep sensitive face. So it was with pride that Crowfoot saw his son strike out northward from camp with his comrades to raid the Crees. But, like Crowfoot's father, the boy did not come back. He was shot and killed when the Crees discovered the small party north of the Red Deer River.

The people loved Crowfoot and, when he suffered such a tragic loss, they mourned with him. He was a rich and generous man, but his role as a family man had been marred by death and disease.

Crowfoot was shocked by the killing of his only healthy son. He mourned, but as he did so the anger burned within him and he called for revenge upon the Crees. Four warriors in his camp heard the plea and volunteered to search the area to the north for an enemy camp. Revenge did not have to be upon the actual killer of Crowfoot's son; it was knowledge enough that the Crees were responsible. The blood of a Cree, any Cree, would avenge the loss.

After being away for several days, the scouts returned with the news that a Cree camp had been found. Crowfoot, ignoring his weak leg, called for volunteers for a revenge party which he personally would lead. The response was immediate, but the chief selected only those who were close friends or relatives. Among the revenge party were the four scouts, his foster brother Three Bulls, a brother-in-law Weasel Calf, Running Rabbit, and Big Road. Others in the party were his younger brother Iron Shield, Bear Galloping, Voice Sounding Afar, Yellow Horse, Chief Calf, Running Among Buffalo, Eagle Sun, Wolf Head, Favorite Child, Wolf Shoe, White Pup, Eagle Tail Feathers, Medicine Bull, Pretty Woman, and Two Horse.[1]

Gathering their best horses, the party was led by Crowfoot, with his foster brother acting as guide. Some time later, as they neared the enemy camp, the revenge party found a small group of Crees on the prairie. On a signal from Crowfoot, they attacked and succeeded in killing one man before the others escaped. This body, which was scalped and mutilated, satisfied Crowfoot's desire for revenge.

Some time after this incident, a peace treaty was made between the Crees and the Blackfeet. This was one of the many short-lived treaties which were instigated by the chiefs and

[1] Interview with Duck Chief by Hanks, about 1939. Of these men, Three Bulls, Running Rabbit, and Yellow Horse later became head chiefs of the tribe, while Weasel Calf and White Pup became minor chiefs.

later broken by the young warriors. Crowfoot, still mourning for his son but always anxious for peace, visited a camp of Crees which had come from the Eagle Hills area. One evening, while resting after a day of visiting, he was awakened by his wife, the one whose boy had died in the recent raid. She told her husband of meeting a young man who bore a remarkable likeness to her dead boy. He was several years older than their lost son, but he had the same handsome face, the same lithe body. It was as though their child had come back from the Sand Hills.

When Crowfoot met the young man, he too was startled by the striking similarity between this Cree and his dead son. In speaking to him, Crowfoot learned that, although he had some relatives, the close members of his family were dead. The chief told the boy of the loss of his only healthy son and invited him to come to the Blackfoot camps. The young man's name was *Pito-kanow-apiwin*, or Poundmaker. When he joined the south-bound party, he became an adopted son of Crowfoot and was given the Blackfoot name *Makoyi-koh-kin*, or Wolf Thin Legs. Crowfoot again had a son.

In temperament, Poundmaker was much like his foster father. His inclinations were toward peace and, like Crowfoot, he was able to foresee the time when his people would live harmoniously with the white men. He was an apt pupil and in the passing months he learned much from the Blackfoot leader. He soon spoke the language fluently and, although there was some hostility and jealousy shown by the Blackfeet, he was accepted as Wolf Thin Legs, son of Crowfoot.

Before long, the peace treaty was shattered by the rumbling hooves of stolen horses and the sharp explosions of muskets. The Crees and Blackfeet again were at war; but Poundmaker remained in Crowfoot's camp and not until later did he return to his people. When he left, Crowfoot made him rich with gifts of horses and other presents and wise with the knowledge of leadership. Poundmaker returned as often as he could during the 1870's, and each time his reputation and wealth grew greater. Crowfoot, who had come to love the Cree as his own son, was happy about the young man's success. He would have liked him to stay forever with the Blackfeet, but he knew of Poundmaker's loneliness for those who spoke the Cree tongue.

In the meantime, the situation on the prairies was changing rapidly. The portion of Blackfoot territory north of the International Boundary had been under British charter to the Hudson's Bay Company since 1670. This knowledge would have surprised and puzzled the Blackfeet, who considered the land to be theirs and not the property of a foreign king or queen. In 1869 negotiations were under way to transfer the entire Hudson's Bay territory, called Rupert's Land, to the custody of the newly formed Dominion of Canada.

The Blackfeet would not have been interested in the proceedings even if someone had tried to explain them. But other people in Blackfoot territory saw the changeover as an opportunity to become rich. The sale of liquor was prohibited in Montana, and those who sold the potent concoctions did so at a great risk. Similarly, liquor was outlawed in the British possession and, as long as the Hudson's Bay Company was in control, it had the authority to stamp out the illicit trade.

Late in 1869 two Montana merchants, John Healy and Alf Hamilton, realized that the land sale was going through and the Hudson's Bay Company no longer would have the right to enforce its laws. At the same time, the Canadian government had taken no steps to administer the area, so the Canadian plains would be in a legal vacuum.

Secure in the knowledge that no one could stop them, the Montana traders built a fort at the confluence of the Oldman and St. Mary rivers, in the heart of the Bloods' hunting grounds, and stocked it with whisky, repeating rifles, and other trade goods. By the spring of 1870, the trade had grossed some fifty thousand dollars and the post had received the descriptive title of Fort Whoop-Up. When news of the success spread among the rest of the Montana traders, there was a rush to invade the Blackfoot territory, and posts like Standoff, Slideout, and Robbers' Roost soon were in business. Whisky and repeating rifles were the two most important items of trade.

The flow of liquor into the territory caused frequent battles between traders and Indians and, more tragically, among the Indians themselves. In one winter, no less than seventy Bloods were killed in drunken quarrels among themselves.[2] Intratribal conflicts, freezing to death while drunk, murder by white traders, starvation because everything had been sold for whisky, and the poisonous effects of the whisky itself all resulted in numerous deaths. But the American traders paid a heavy price in blood for their buffalo robes. At least four trading posts were destroyed by Indians, and almost all were attacked on various occasions by the drunken or angry Blackfoot warriors.[3] The whisky forts which were closest to Crowfoot's hunting grounds were Spitzee Post on the Highwood River, Lafayette French's Post at Blackfoot Crossing, and Elbow River Post at the confluence of the Bow and Elbow rivers.[4]

[2] Donald Graham, "Donald Graham's Narrative of 1872–73" (ed. by Hugh A. Dempsey), *Alberta Historical Review*, Winter, 1956, 17.
[3] In the *Helena* (Montana) *Weekly Herald*, March 14, 1872, a correspondent described the conditions at Fort Whoop-Up and said seven traders had been killed during the winter. These included "Gilpoich, killed by a Blood Indian in camp near Healy's Fort, on Belly River . . . Jack Wade, also killed by Blood Indians on Belly River . . . 'Cut-Lip' Jack killed by Piegans . . . Pete Cobel, a half-breed, was killed in a camp by Piegans . . . Baptiste Musha, Half-breed, was killed by Blood Indians in camp; was formerly bullwhacker in the Diamond R. Train. In every instance the parties were either directly or indirectly engaged in the trade of whiskey to Indians."
[4] This last is within the present city limits of Calgary.

Crowfoot's attitude toward the traders was similar to that of the Hudson's Bay men, who also had sold liquor until it was outlawed in the 1860's. If the American traders respected him and treated his people fairly, he considered them to be his friends. Others who cheated the Blackfeet were condemned by the chief, who advised his followers not to trade at their posts. But, like other chiefs of the nation, he was powerless to stamp out the whisky trade and the evil he knew it was causing his people.

Crowfoot was not averse to drinking liquor and was a regular visitor to some of the forts. While not a continuous or frequently heavy drinker, he was known to get drunk on occasion; it was then he was subject to his more violent outbursts of temper. In later years, when liquor was no longer easily available to Indians, he made no attempt to obtain it by illicit means but instead was instrumental in keeping whisky peddlers away from his people.

While the Blackfeet usually went to the trading posts with their buffalo robes, some of the more enterprising traders came to their camps.[5] On one occasion traders arrived at a large camp of Bloods and Blackfeet and, when Crowfoot heard about them, he sent one of his young men over to buy some whisky. When the man reached the wagon, he found some Indians threatening the traders, shooting holes in their kegs, and pillaging their robes. The young man immediately rode back to his camp and told Crowfoot of the trouble. The chief seized his whip and hurried over to the wagon, where he ordered the troublemakers away.

"If you people are going to trade," he told them, "you must be fair."[6]

[5] Philip Weinard, "Early High River and the Whiskey Traders," *Alberta Historical Review*, Summer, 1956, 13.
[6] Interview with Duck Chief by Hanks, about 1939.

Most of the pillagers left the traders alone, but, when a few ignored Crowfoot, he struck at them with his whip. Then, as he was swinging it, a Blood grabbed the whip from his hand and threw it away. When the Blood mounted his horse, Crowfoot called out to his men to stop him and then rode up and struck the troublemaker, took away his blankets, and chastized him for attacking the traders.

By early 1874, the disastrous effects of the whisky trade were visible in every Blackfoot camp. A priest who visited the tribe in the spring of that year noted that where "formerly they had been the most opulent Indians in the country ... now they were clothed in rags, without horses and without guns."[7] Completely demoralized and powerless to act, many older men felt that the whole nation would be destroyed by the white men through a combination of liquor, murder, and disease. Others viewed with alarm the more frequent incursions of Cree and mixed-blood hunting parties into Blackfoot territory. Not directly affected by the whisky trade, these traditional enemies were taking advantage of the situation to whittle down the size of the Blackfoot hunting grounds.

The whole tragic situation had frequently been brought to the attention of Canadian government officials by the Hudson's Bay Company, missionaries, and men who had been commissioned to examine the territory after its transfer from Britain in 1870. The repeated evidences of debauchery and murder and the construction of trading posts by American citizens on Canadian soil finally could not be ignored. Therefore, in 1873 the North West Mounted Police was organized to set up military-style posts and to bring the queen's law to the western prairies.

[7] Constantine Scollen, priest, to Lieutenant Governor Alexander Morris, September 8, 1876, in Alexander Morris, *The Treaties of Canada with the Indians of Manitoba and the North-West Territories*, 248.

CHAPTER SEVEN

THE RED COATS

While the North West Mounted Police were preparing to cross the plains from Manitoba to the Blackfoot territory, officials wanted to notify the Indians that they were coming. The matter was referred to the North West Territories Council and the Reverend John McDougall, a Methodist missionary, was chosen to undertake the task. As soon as he received the message in the summer of 1874, McDougall set out for the Blackfoot Crossing. There he met a party of Indians who told him that Crowfoot and Old Sun were camped together about twelve miles north. These Indians had just come from that camp and were on their way to a whisky fort at the Crossing.

Next morning, the missionary sent word by the returning Indians that he would visit the camp during the day to deliver a message from the queen. After the messengers had left, McDougall and his small party followed the trail along Crowfoot Creek until the huge combined camp came into view. It was in a wide valley where a plentiful supply of grass ensured good feeding for the horses. Crowfoot now camped farther south than he had a few years earlier; the frequent raids by Crees upon the whisky-weakened camps had forced him to remain in the heart of his hunting grounds.

Approaching the camp, the missionary saw that the Blackfoot messengers had brought a large supply of whisky to the lodges. There were sounds of singing and drumming echoing along the valley, while drunken laughter came from some of the tipis.

Moving through the camp to the Moccasin band, McDougall

saw that all was quiet near Crowfoot's lodge. There he was invited inside and was introduced to the great chieftain. Crowfoot heard the missionary explain that a party of red-coated police was crossing the plains from the east and would build forts within Blackfoot hunting grounds. He learned that the police were sent by the queen to stop the traders from selling liquor and to keep the Indians from killing each other. He was told of British justice and that any man, whether Indian or white, would receive equal treatment if guilty of a crime. When McDougall finished, Crowfoot took the missionary's hand, placed it over his own heart, and said:

My brother, your words make me glad. I listened to them not only with my ears, but with my heart also. In the coming of the Long Knives,[1] with their firewater and their quick-shooting guns, we are weak, and our people have been woefully slain and impoverished. You say this will be stopped. We are glad to have it stopped. We want peace. What you tell us about this strong power which will govern with good law and treat the Indian the same as the white man makes us glad to hear. My brother, I believe you, and am thankful.[2]

As the other chiefs in his lodge arose to express their agreement, Crowfoot knew he could assure the missionary that the

[1] Americans. This term may have originated with the swords carried by early traders and soldiers.

[2] John McDougall, On Western Trails in the Early Seventies, 184. In a report to Richard Hardisty, the missionary gave a slightly different account of Crowfoot's speech. He wrote, "If left to ourselves we are gone. The whiskey brought among us by the Traders is fast killing us off and we are powerless before the evil. [We are] totally unable to resist the temptation to drink when brought in contact with the white man's water. We are also unable to pitch anywhere that the Trader cannot follow us. Our horses, Buffalo robes and other articles of trade go for whiskey, a large number of our people have killed one another and perished in various ways under the influence, and now that we hear of our Great Mother sending her soldiers into our country for our good we are glad." (McDougall to Hardisty, October 20, 1874, in the Alexander Morris Papers at the Public Archives of Manitoba, Winnipeg.)

coming of the Mounted Police would be a peaceful event. He had seen the need for such a force to help his people escape from the vicious liquor traffic and was quick to offer his co-operation.

When the police arrived in Blackfoot country late in 1874, they chose a site for a fort on the Oldman River. The first chief to visit them was Crowfoot's foster brother, Three Bulls, sent there on Crowfoot's instructions to test McDougall's words about equality for the Indian and the white man. Three Bulls reported to the commander, Colonel James F. Macleod, that two American traders were operating an illicit post at Pine Coulee, about fifty miles north. As proof, he swore he had exchanged two horses for two gallons of whisky. A short time later, the chief led the police to Pine Coulee, and both traders were arrested. Crowfoot had ample evidence of the sincerity of the police when he learned they had destroyed the liquor and confiscated more than a hundred buffalo robes, ten guns, and sixteen horses. The men were fined up to two hundred dollars each and one who was unable to pay was sentenced to a jail term.[3]

During November, Colonel Macleod sent word through interpreter Jerry Potts that he wanted to meet the chiefs of the Blackfoot nation. The first to respond were leaders of the Bloods and North Piegans, both of whom normally camped in the area. It was not until the last week in November that a message was brought from Crowfoot. A young man appeared at the fort and announced that the Blackfoot tribe was coming down from the Bow River. Crowfoot had been told the police were their friends, but the messenger had been sent ahead to obtain assurances of trust to take back to the chief.

On December 1, Crowfoot and his people arrived at Fort Macleod. With Potts acting as interpreter, the chief visited the

[3] Samuel B. Steele, *Forty Years in Canada*, 77–78.

fort and met Colonel Macleod and other officers. He then requested that a general council be held so that the police officer could explain his presence in their territory and guarantee his friendship with the Blackfoot people. Later, Crowfoot and several other chiefs were invited to a grand council, where they heard Macleod explain why the queen had sent the police into their country and how the laws would be enforced. He repeated McDougall's assertion that there would be only one law for everyone and that both Indians and white men would be punished for breaking it. No one had to be afraid of being punished for anything he did not know was wrong, but all Indians were expected to respect the laws which the police had made. There was a nod of approval among the chiefs when he said that they had not come to steal the land from the Indians, but only to protect the people who were in it.

When the speech was finished, Crowfoot shook hands with the colonel and the other white men in the room. He then bared his right arm and with graceful gestures he made an eloquent speech thanking the Sun and the queen for sending the police to save his people from the whisky traders.

From this first meeting, there was a feeling of friendship and trust between Crowfoot and Macleod. Although they were from two different worlds, each recognized the qualities of the other. Both had the same desires for peace and each proved that once his word was given it never would be broken.

In the months that followed, Crowfoot displayed his willingness to work with the police. In the spring of 1875 he attended the trials of two Indians at the fort and was impressed with the honesty and impartiality of the courts. He approved the plan to halt intertribal warfare and made a real effort to live at peace with his enemies. Although he had favored such action before the arrival of the Mounted Police, only in isolated cases had he been able to act with any measure of success.

But, with the old order changing, he emerged as Crowfoot the peacemaker. The stealing of enemy horses was discouraged, and the chief did everything within his power to keep the young men off the warpath.

In the next few years, there were many times when Crowfoot returned stolen horses to their rightful owners. In one case a war party returned with horses stolen from the Crees. Crowfoot sent two men to recover them and notified the Crees to come and get them. The chief then held the horses until they were picked up.[4] In another instance, some horses were taken from the Stonies. Crowfoot again interceded and sent two men to the enemy camp to return the animals.

His actions were resented in some circles, particularly the younger warrior groups, but only on rare occasion was he defied. If this occurred, he sometimes took a horse from his own herd and sent it to the person who had been robbed. This not only added to Crowfoot's own prestige but reflected upon the poor character of the warrior who had defied him.

With the whisky forts closed and the sale of liquor suppressed, a rapid change took place among the Blackfeet. Where the lodges had been tattered and worn, they now were fresh and new. Much-needed clothing was made from hides which previously had gone for whisky. There was harmony in the camps, and within less than two years the Blackfeet had purchased more than two thousand horses to replace the ones they had sold to whisky traders.[5]

In the summer of 1875, Crowfoot visited the Reverend John McDougall and said he was pleased with the progress his people had made. He had found the police to be honest, and British justice was all that it was promised to be. But Crowfoot, with keen foresight, had a problem he wanted the missionary

[4] Interview with Duck Chief by Hanks, about 1939.
[5] Morris, *Treaties*, 248.

to solve. Now that peace had come to his people's hunting grounds, the white men were starting to move in. There was only a handful, but he knew it was just the beginning. There were fewer buffalo than there had been ten years ago and some day there might be none. What would the future hold for the Blackfeet? That was his question. What would become of them and their vast lands?

McDougall explained in detail what had happened to the Indians in other parts of Canada. Treaties had been signed, lands set aside, and the rights of the Indians respected. He told the chief that "in due time treaties would be made and a settled condition created in this country wherein justice would be given to all."[6] This was Crowfoot's first intimation of a Canadian treaty, and he seemed satisfied. He knew his tribe could not always hold its hunting grounds against the advancing white civilization but was worried that a settlement might not be made.

A few weeks later, when traveling near Blackfoot Crossing, Crowfoot was told that a party of police had been sighted nearby. Riding over to their wagons, he met the commander of the Canadian Militia, Major General E. Selby-Smyth, who was making a special tour of the West for his government. That evening, when the party had camped, Crowfoot held a council with Smyth and asked him to enlarge upon the question of treaties. The general explained he was not in a position to speak for the queen on that question but promised to carry the inquiry back to Ottawa with him on his return journey. He stressed that his government's objective was to deal fairly with all tribes in Her Majesty's domain and to extend uniform justice to the Indians of the plains.[7]

[6] McDougall, *Opening the Great West*, 15–16.
[7] Report of E. Selby-Smyth to the Minister of Justice. In *Sessional Papers of Canada*, 1876, No. 7, xxix–xxx.

This satisfied Crowfoot and his council, although they would have liked a more definite answer. Therefore, in the autumn of 1875, Crowfoot called a large council meeting of Blackfeet, Bloods, and Piegans to discuss the land question and to submit a memorial to the queen's government protesting the increasing invasion of their country by mixed-bloods and whites. When the meeting was called fifteen chiefs, including all five head chiefs from the three tribes, were present. The problems and grievances were discussed and, with the help of a white renegade who lived in Crowfoot's camp, a memorial was prepared.[8] It was a remarkable document drafted by a group of leaders who had fought other battles with knives and now were trying white man's methods to obtain justice. Entitled a

[8] Morris Papers, No. 1265. This document was prepared by the renegade Jean L'Heureux "at the request & behalf of the Blackfeet Indian Chiefs." The fifteen chiefs signing it were Crowfoot, Old Sun, Eagle, and Low Horn for the Blackfeet; Bull Back Fat, Bad Head, Red Crow, Many Spotted Horses, and White Striped Dog for the Bloods; and Sitting on an Eagle Tail, Walking Forward, and *Stakkas* for the North Piegans.

L'Heureux was born near St. Hyacinthe, Quebec, in about 1825 and studied for the priesthood. Before completing his studies he was involved in some criminal activities and was expelled. He went west to the Montana gold fields in about 1859, and after a short period there he made a cassock and passed himself off as a priest at the Jesuit mission on Sun River. When the truth was discovered and he was caught in homosexual activities, he already had gained the friendship of many Blackfeet. He moved to their camps and drifted northward into Alberta, where he went to the St. Albert mission. He succeeded in convincing the Oblates that he was a priest and, by the time news of his true identity came from Montana, he had been seen so often with the priests that the Indians never could be convinced he was an imposter. L'Heureux then moved to Crowfoot's camp and remained with the Indians until they settled on their reserve. During this time he performed marriages, baptized children, and performed all the rites of a priest. He also acted as interpreter and scribe for the chiefs. In about 1880, L'Heureux became interpreter for the Indian Department but was dismissed in 1891 for his continued religious work. Throughout his life he was a controversial figure, despised and distrusted by many fur traders, an asset and embarrassment to the Oblates, and received by the Blackfeet with the mixed emotions they had for crazy people. After his dismissal from his interpreter's position, he became a recluse near Pincher Creek and finally died in Lacombe Home near Calgary on March 19, 1919.

petition "of the *Chokitapix*[9] or Blackfeet Indians," it was given to the commanding officer of the newly built Fort Calgary for transmission to Lieutenant Governor Alexander Morris. In it, the Blackfeet set out the major problems confronting the nation.

They complained that

> white men have already taken the best locations and built houses in any place they pleased in your petitioners' hunting grounds; that the Half-breeds and Cree Indians hunt buffalo, summer and winter, in the centre of the hunting grounds of the Blackfeet nation since 4 years [ago]; that American traders and others are forming large settlements on Belly River, the best winter hunting grounds of your petitioners,

and, finally, that "no Indian Commissioner has been seen by us."

The council asked that a commissioner "visit us this summer at the Hand Hills and [state] the time of his arrival there, so we could meet with him and hold a Council for putting a [stop] to the invasion of our Country, till our Treaty be made with the Government." The petitioners were "perfectly willing the Mounted Police and the Missionaries remain in our Country, for we are indebted to them for important services." They also asked for the removal of American traders and that the Hudson's Bay Company build a post to replace them. The petition concluded by saying "that your petitioners feel perfectly confident the representative of our Great Mother, Her Majesty the Queen, will do justice to her Indian children."

In 1876, the news was circulated among the Blackfeet that a treaty was being made with the Crees. This brought grumblings from the chiefs, who felt that the Crees were receiving preferential treatment. Perhaps the Blackfeet did not want a

[9] Literally, "Prairie People."

treaty like the one the Crees were signing, but they did want to meet with the queen's representatives and come to an understanding about the problems outlined in their petition.

McDougall heard their complaints and advised Crowfoot to sent a delegation to visit the commissioners while they were negotiating the Cree treaty. He also sent an appeal to Lieutenant Governor Morris explaining the situation in Blackfoot country.[10] Following the missionary's advice, the chief dispatched two delegates early in October, 1876, to meet the commissioners at Fort Pitt. Traveling lightly and expecting to find game along the route, the two men set out. However, after several days of difficult travel north of Hand Hills, they were forced to turn back. But the sentiments of the Blackfeet were adequately delivered to the commissioner by McDougall and by Constantine Scollen, an Oblate priest. Governor Morris agreed that the good relations between the Blackfeet and whites should be maintained and that it would be dangerous to delay the treaty. He therefore announced that "steps should be taken for the making of a treaty, early next season at some central place, where the Blackfeet are in the habit of assembling in early summer."[11]

This news was sent to the Blackfoot nation and was received with mixed emotions. Some were in favor of it, but others, particularly some of the Bloods, did not approve of negotiating for a treaty. Rather, they wanted to discuss their grievances and find solutions to the encroachment on their lands. Some of the southern leaders who had participated in the American treaty in 1855 believed that such agreements were worthless, as they had seen how one promise after another was broken.

[10] John McDougall to Lieutenant Governor Morris, September 8, 1876, in the Indian Affairs Archives at Ottawa.

[11] Lieutenant Governor Morris to the Minister of the Interior, October 24, 1876, loc. cit.

Crowfoot, who had no experience with American treaties, believed that the queen would honor her agreements. He trusted Colonel Macleod and others who advised him but would not support any treaty negotiations unless the conditions and terms were to the advantage of his people.

CHAPTER EIGHT

SITTING BULL SPURNED

The Sioux, whose vast hunting grounds were spread through the Dakotas, always had been enemies of the Blackfoot nation. They did not meet often, but, when they did, it was with gunfire and war cries.

It is doubtful if Crowfoot ever had met the Sioux in the early years; only the Bloods and South Piegans encountered them in southern Montana. But he had heard of their bloody battles with the American soldiers and of their war to drive the gold seekers from the Black Hills.

The Laramie Treaty of 1868 had given the Sioux hunting rights in a large area of the Dakotas north of the North Platte River and east of the Big Horn Mountains. No white men were allowed to trade or travel in that area as long as there was hunting for the tribes. But in 1874, when gold was discovered, hundreds of prospectors ignored the treaty and poured into the Black Hills area. The Sioux appealed to the government to honor its agreement, but, instead, soldiers sent in to protect the miners. The inevitable attacks on the gold seekers followed, and at the end of 1875 the Sioux were ordered to leave the area and go to their allotted reservations. When they refused, the army made plans for a major campaign in the spring.

In March, General George Crook attacked a large camp of Sioux and Cheyennes on the Powder River, destroying the lodges and forcing the Indians to withdraw to Montana territory. This action made a large number of Sioux decide to go peacefully to their reservation to avoid further conflict. But most of the others drifted farther west into the Big Horn Mountains, awaiting the conflict they knew would come.

In an effort to amass a large force to meet the soldiers, Sioux chief Sitting Bull sent runners to all the Sioux and Cheyenne camps. He told them that, if they united in this common cause, they would destroy the Long Knives within their territory. After the Sioux had been notified, runners were sent farther afield, to allies and enemies alike, urging them to join the coming struggle. To the northwest, runners were sent to the Piegans, the Bloods, and to the camp of Crowfoot.

Late in May, the messenger arrived and presented Crowfoot with a gift of tobacco. He said he was from Sitting Bull, the great Hunkpapa chief, and brought the tobacco as a peace offering and invitation to cross the boundary into the United States to join the Sioux in their fight against the Americans. The Blackfeet were promised plenty of horses and mules captured from the Americans, and white women prisoners. The messenger said that after the Americans and Crows had been defeated, the Sioux would come to Canada with the Blackfeet and exterminate the whites. The red-coated soldiers were weak, he said, and it would take only a short time to destroy their police forts.

Crowfoot flatly rejected the idea of going to war, either against the American soldiers or the Mounted Police, but before answering the courier he sent his own runners to determine the feelings of the Bloods and Piegans. When he confirmed that their hatred of the Sioux was still strong, he sent a Blackfoot messenger to tell Sitting Bull that his people would not join the Sioux crusade. When the messenger returned a few weeks later, he reported that the Sioux had gathered a large force and soon would attack the American soldiers. They had told the runner that, after the soldiers were defeated, the Sioux would come to Canada and not only destroy the Mounted

Police but wipe out the Blackfeet for refusing to join them. The messenger had come to Crowfoot's camp with this disturbing news at the same time as a Mounted Police inspector, Cecil Denny, had arrived from Fort Calgary on a patrol.[1] Crowfoot invited the policeman to his lodge and explained the whole situation to him. He knew the Sioux were a large nation and asked if the Mounted Police could be counted on to support the Blackfeet if they were attacked. Denny replied that the Blackfeet were subjects of the queen and could always expect the protection of the police. Crowfoot was satisfied with the news and responded that his people also would help the whites. He would send two thousand warriors into battle if the Sioux ever attacked the police.

After making this generous offer, Crowfoot revealed for the first time that he had some concept of the bleak future in store for his people. His keen intelligence enabled him to assess the events taking place around him and to realize that the new life would be a difficult one. In that year of 1876 probably no other Indian and very few white men in Blackfoot country saw the situation as clearly as Crowfoot.

> We all see that the day is coming when the buffalo will all be killed, and we shall have nothing more to live on . . . then you will come into our camp and see the poor Blackfoot starving. I know that the heart of the White soldier will be sorry for

[1] Cecil Denny was an original member of the North West Mounted Police who came west in 1874. After leaving the force he served as Indian agent to the Blackfeet, Stonies, and Sarcees in 1882–83 and was special agent for the Indian commissioner during the Riel Rebellion of 1885. In later years, a distant relative died and he became Sir Cecil Denny, sixth baronet of Tralee Castle. Throughout his years in the West he was a controversial figure who had the complete trust of the Indians but was disliked by many government officials because of his outspoken manner, unorthodox procedures, and free and easy ways. His name was mentioned by the prime minister in 1885 and a possible Indian commissioner. (John A. Macdonald to Edgar Dewdney, November 16, 1885, in the Macdonald Papers at the Public Archives of Canada in Ottawa.) Denny died in Edmonton, August 24, 1928.

89

us, and they will tell the great mother who will not let her children starve.

We are getting shut in. The Crees are coming in to our country from the north, and the white men from the south and east, and they are all destroying our means of living; but still, although we plainly see these days coming, we will not join the Sioux against the whites, but will depend upon you to help us.[2]

When Denny made his report, the officials in the national capital were so impressed that a copy of Crowfoot's speech was sent to Queen Victoria. The secretary of state for the colonies replied:

Her Majesty has commanded me to instruct you to inform the Chiefs of the tribe that Her Majesty has heard, with much satisfaction, of their faithful conduct in declining to take up arms with the Sioux Indians, and has been much gratified by this evidence of their loyalty and attachment . . . .[3]

By the time Crowfoot had discussed the situation with the police, General George A. Custer already had been killed when he attacked the Sioux camps on the Little Bighorn. Two hundred and sixty-five soldiers, including three Crow scouts, died on that fateful June day. From the scene of the battle the Sioux scattered, with Sitting Bull's followers going north into the Milk River country. In November the first Sioux lodges moved into the Wood Mountain district, east of Cypress Hills, and by the end of the year several thousand Sioux were camped on Canadian soil. They were east of Blackfoot country, but their presence was immediately known to Crowfoot and the other leaders. By this time, the chief realized the Sioux were fleeing from the American soldiers and the threat of an attack from them was slim.

[2] *Sessional Papers of Canada*, 1877, No. 9, 23–24.
[3] *Ibid.*

By early 1877, most of the refugee Sioux had entered Canada and were camped between the Cypress Hills and Wood Mountain. In March, Sitting Bull led the remainder of his followers into the territory and assured the Mounted Police that he would remain peaceful.

The buffalo herds had been growing steadily smaller, and in that year the main herds were farther east than usual. The Sioux were well provided for, but their invasion and the destruction of the buffalo was watched with anger and distrust by the surrounding tribes. When Crowfoot led his band on the spring hunt, he was forced to travel far to the east and did not find any large herds until almost in the Cypress Hills. There, although dangerously close to the Sioux, he kept his warriors at peace and would not let them raid the enemy camps.

Sitting Bull, realizing that his stay in Canada hinged upon his ability to keep peace, learned of the Blackfoot camp. He knew Crowfoot had influence with the police and of all the chiefs he was the most favorably inclined toward peace. Therefore, late in the spring Sitting Bull sent a gift of tobacco and other articles, indicating his desire for friendship and peace.[4] Crowfoot did not refuse the tobacco but would not smoke until he learned more about the intentions of the Sioux chief.

A short time later, when Crowfoot was camped in the Great Sand Hills north of Cypress Hills, he was told that a Sioux peace mission was approaching. The warriors were invited into the camp and Crowfoot was surprised to learn that Sitting Bull himself was among them; he had come to visit and make peace. The two men shook hands and exchanged tobacco. Pipes were produced and, for the first time, Crowfoot consented to speak with the Sioux chief. A long discussion was held between the two men and an immediate friendship was established. The Blackfoot and Sioux held a friendship dance

[4] *Fort Benton* (Montana) *Record*, August 24, 1877.

CROWFOOT

in the camp before the Sioux returned south later in the day.[5]
There was some consternation among the whites, particularly the Americans, when they learned of this conference.
Montanans feared "that Sitting Bull is making the greatest
exertions to effect an alliance with all the Indians of the North"
and was showing his "readiness to co-operate with any of the
tribes who desire to join him in another campaign of slaughter and destruction."[6]

But the meeting between Crowfoot and Sitting Bull had
been for peace, not war. In his precarious position, the Sioux
chief could not afford another campaign. And Crowfoot saw
no reason to fight.

[5] G. H. Gooderham, Indian agent, Blackfoot Reserve, to W. S. Campbell
(Stanley Vestal), Norman, Oklahoma, September 6, 1930. Gooderham obtained the information from High Eagle, a relative of Crowfoot, who was
present at the meeting. A copy of the letter, provided by Mr. Gooderham,
is in the author's possession.
[6] *Fort Benton Record*, August 24, 1877.

92

CHAPTER NINE

THE BLACKFOOT TREATY

In August, 1877, Lieutenant Governor David Laird and Colonel Macleod were appointed as commissioners to negotiate a treaty with the Blackfeet and other tribes in the area. The government was anxious to complete the last treaty on the Canadian plains to formalize its friendship with the Blackfeet and to leave them with no reasons for joining the hostile Sioux. In addition, a few cattle had been introduced into the area, and settlers already were eying the rich grasslands. To the north, Cree and mixed-blood hunters were encroaching farther and farther into Blackfoot lands, knowing that the Mounted Police would offer them protection. Meanwhile, in eastern Canada the need for a transcontinental railway to bring the nation together had been discussed for several years and surveyors were beginning to look for possible routes across the prairies. As Crowfoot had predicted, his tribe was being pressed from all sides. Perhaps some of the warriors in the nation wanted to drive out the intruders, but Crowfoot hoped that a fair treaty would give them all the protection they needed.

The date of September 17 was set for the treaty meeting, which would take place at Fort Macleod. When Colonel Macleod received his instructions, he sent messages to the chiefs of the Blackfeet, Bloods, North Piegans, Sarcees, and Stonies, telling them of the time and place.

Crowfoot, who previously had stated that the Hand Hills area in the north was a suitable meeting place, sent word that he would not attend if the negotiations were to be held in a white man's fort. He insisted that the site be farther north in his own area. The subject was discussed by the commissioners and, reluctantly, the meeting place was changed to Blackfoot Crossing.[1]

The chiefs of the Bloods and North Piegans were angry about the change, claiming that Fort Macleod was central to all tribes while the Crossing was within only Crowfoot's domain. When told that no further changes would be made, several of the Blood chiefs announced that they would not be present.

With the Indian situation still explosive on the Montana frontier, settlers at Fort Benton predicted grave troubles because of Crowfoot's stand. "This will cause great dissatisfaction among the Bloods and North Piegans," the *Fort Benton Record* predicted, "and an outbreak is feared at the place where the treaty is to be held."[2]

Although the situation did not appear this serious, the Mounted Police realized that undue dissension could interfere with the negotiations. All leading chiefs within the area would need to agree with the terms of the treaty before it could be ratified. So, in the period immediately prior to the meeting, the police used all their persuasive powers to induce the reluctant chiefs to attend.

One of the underlying causes of the dissension was the false position in which the Mounted Police and other officials placed Crowfoot in regard to the negotiations. Crowfoot was considered by them to be the head chief of the whole nation and the undisputed leader not only of the Blackfeet but also of the Bloods and the Piegans. Such a thought was entirely foreign to the Blackfeet, with the result that chiefs with equal or greater influence than Crowfoot felt they were being ignored. Red

---

1 *Fort Benton Record*, August 24, 1877, and Morris, *Treaties*, 251.
2 *Fort Benton Record*, August 24, 1877.

Crow and Rainy Chief, the two head chiefs of the Bloods, had followings which were larger than Crowfoot's, and Red Crow in particular wielded a greater authority in tribal decisions. But, because he did not have the diplomatic reputation of the Blackfoot chief, nor had he established such peaceful relations, he had gone relatively unnoticed. The distinction between the Blackfoot tribe and the Blackfoot nation also was a confusing factor; when some officials were told that Crowfoot was the leader of the Blackfeet, they believed this to be of the whole nation, not just a part of one tribe. With the European concept of kings with absolute authority, they could not conceive of the democratic type of native leadership which provided for no all-powerful superleader.

Crowfoot was aware of this misunderstanding and, although he usually saw that his fellow chiefs were consulted, there were times when the robe of supreme commander did not feel at all uncomfortable on his shoulders.

By the middle of September the Indians began drifting in to Blackfoot Crossing. They took their allotted places, and soon the sounds of singing and drumming echoed across the valley. Medicine pipe ceremonies and social dances were held among the allied tribes as they waited for the commissioners.

On September 16 the government treaty party arrived and was greeted by Crowfoot and his fellow chiefs. The officials were disturbed to see that few North Piegans and practically no Bloods were camped in the flats. Only the Blackfeet were on the south side, while the enemy Stonies were camped with the missionary McDougall on the north. No word had been received from Red Crow, head chief of the Bloods. In the hopes that he would soon arrive, the commissioners made arrangements for a brief meeting on the seventeenth and requested a delay of two days.

Commissioner David Laird announced also that rations of

flour, tea, sugar, tobacco, and beef would be provided to the Indians during the negotiations. Anyone who needed food was advised to apply to the police. Although the Stonies and one Blood minor chief asked for food, Crowfoot refused to accept any rations until he had heard the terms of the treaty. "Though I feared this refusal did not augur well for the final success of the negotiations," reported Laird, "yet I could not help wishing that other Indians whom I have seen, had a little of the spirit in regard to dependence upon the Government exhibited on this occasion by the great Chief of the Blackfeet."[3]

On Wednesday afternoon when the meeting again was called, the ranks included the Blackfeet, a few Bloods, North Piegans, Stonies, and Sarcees, but the leading chiefs of the Bloods still were absent. However, not wishing to delay any longer, Commissioner Laird outlined the terms of the proposed treaty and pointed out the situation which existed.

> In a very few years, the buffalo will probably be all destroyed, and for this reason the queen wishes to help you to live in the future in some other way. She wishes you to allow her white children to come and live on your land and raise cattle, and should you agree to this she will assist you to raise cattle and grain, and thus give you the means of living when the buffalo are no more. She will also pay you and your children money every year, which you can spend as you please.

His entire speech was a long one and gave full details of the queen's offer. She wanted them to allow the white men to live on their hunting grounds; in return she would give them a piece of land, cattle, potatoes, five dollars annual treaty money, and ammunition.

After the meeting each tribe went into council. Among the Blackfeet, the gatherings were held in the lodge of Heavy

[3] *Ibid.,* 256.

Shield, a brother of Old Sun. There was considerable feeling about the offer; some were in favor of the terms, but most were against them.

There was one statement of the commissioner which they did not like: ". . . in a very few years the buffalo will probably be all destroyed, and for this reason the queen wishes to help you to live in the future in some other way." In that year the buffalo were plentiful, but far to the south, where the white man had been allowed to settle, they were all gone. To the Blackfeet, giving up the land was giving up the buffalo. And to do that was to die.

In the tribal council, Old Sun announced that he was too old to decide for his people. Turning to Crowfoot, he said, "You are used to dealing with the white people. I will abide by your decision."[4]

Eagle Calf, leader of the Many Children band, was the only chief in favor of immediately accepting the treaty. "The whites are coming anyway," he said, "so we might as well have something for our land."[5] But he was alone in his stand; even his own band was against him.

The strongest opponent to the signing was Eagle Ribs. As leader of the Skunks band, he commanded some of the best warriors in the tribe. He was not only against signing but threatened to withdraw with his following unless better terms were made.

As the discussions continued among the chiefs and through the camps, all eyes turned to Crowfoot. Every tribe knew of his influence in the councils of the whites. Besides that, his first loyalty was to his people and his decision would be looked upon with respect.

During this time, Crowfoot was giving the terms his serious

4 Interview with Heavy Shield, March 8, 1957.
5 Interview with Many Guns by Hanks, about 1939.

consideration. He knew that the Mounted Police had saved his tribe from destruction from the whisky traders and he trusted the words of Colonel Macleod. He did not really want to give up the land, to see the mixed-bloods swarm in and kill the buffalo, or to have the whites come in with their herds of cattle and drive the buffalo away. Rather, he wanted to keep the land and, as long as there were buffalo, to let his people have the exclusive right to hunt them. He wanted to welcome the white people but not let them come in unchecked. He had heard the words of the commissioner about giving the Indians their own cattle and farming implements, but he could not see the Blackfeet scratching the earth while the buffalo still wandered the plains.

On the other hand, he knew the buffalo were disappearing and that more and more white people were settling in his land. Some day the buffalo would be gone and his people would starve. That would be the time they would need to rely on the white man for help. Crowfoot saw all sides of the treaty question and believed that the terms generally were favorable to his people. But this was an important decision which should involve all of the chiefs of the Blackfoot nation. In particular, Crowfoot wanted the opinion of Red Crow, head chief of the Bloods, for he had a large following and was greatly respected in the nation. His relationship with Crowfoot also was a personal one, for his sister was one of the wives of the Blackfoot chief.[6] So Crowfoot decided to delay the negotiations until the Bloods arrived and the nation was united.

[6] A. G. Irvine, Blood Indian agent, to Indian commissioner, Regina, August 4, 1892: "I have the honor to enclose herewith Transfer papers for a woman named 'Paper Woman' who wishes to be transferred from the Blackfeet to the Bloods. She is a Blood woman and sister to Head Chief 'Red Crow.' She was married to chief 'Crowfoot' of the Blackfeet, and now wishes to return to her people." (Correspondence from Blood Indian Reserve and Treaty Seven, 1880–1900, copies of extracts in author's possession; hereafter referred to as "Blood Correspondence.")

On Thursday, the council again convened at the official tent. Commissioner Laird clarified a few points about hunting rights and reaffirmed the faithfulness of the queen and her servants. But obviously the Blackfeet were not ready to give a decision. Both Crowfoot and Old Sun arose briefly to say they would not speak that day; they would wait until Friday.

The only speaker was Medicine Calf, war chief of the Bloods.[7] He had signed the treaty with the American government in 1855 and had seen it repeatedly broken by the whites. While he gave credit to the Mounted Police for their work, he deplored the fact that no payment had been made for timber used or destroyed by them and by white settlers in their hunting grounds. All other white people before them had paid for timber rights; why not the police and their friends?

> The Great Mother sent you to this country, and we hope she will be good to us for many years. . . . The Americans gave at first large bags of flour, sugar, and many blankets; the next year it was only half the quantity, and the following years it grew less and less, and now they give only a handful of flour.
>
> We want to get fifty dollars for the Chiefs and thirty dollars each for all the others, men, women and children, and we want the same every year for the future. We want to be paid for all the timber that the police and whites have used since they first came to our country. If it continues to be used as it is, there will soon be no firewood left for the Indians. I hope, Great Father, that you will give us all this that we ask.

This speech, which apparently voiced the sympathies of a number of Indians, had a great deal of thought behind it and was intended as a counter offer to the government. However, its significance, particularly the firewood clause, was missed by Commissioner Laird, who dismissed it with ridicule. "Why,

---

[7] Although commonly known as Button Chief, he signed the treaty under his other name of Medicine Calf.

you Indians ought to pay us for sending these traders in fire-water away and giving you security and peace," he scoffed, "rather than we pay you for the timber used."[8]

This war chief was the only person who publicly opposed the government during the treaty discussions. All other arguments were carried on in the privacy of the council lodges, with the intention of making a unified decision before presenting it to the commissioners.

By the end of the day, the only chief who appeared to openly favor the treaty was Bearspaw, leader of the enemy Stonies. The Blackfeet had been silent and the few Bloods present had been opposed.

That evening the council meetings continued in the camps. The arguments had become heated and the disturbing rumor was circulated that some of the North Piegan warriors wanted to wipe out the commission.[9] But any such move was discouraged by Crowfoot, who continued to wait until the arrival of the other chiefs. This delaying action and the apparent boycotting of the negotiations by the Bloods left a heavy burden on Crowfoot's shoulders. He could feel the pressure of some of the people who, anxious to share in the presents, wanted him to accept immediately. He knew also that a few of the chiefs, particularly the war chiefs, were violently opposed and if he waited too long they could start trouble against the commissioners.

In the meantime, Eagle Calf continued to speak in favor of the agreement. He rode through the camp, proclaiming his

[8] At this point Lieutenant Governor Morris gave an incorrect account of the proceedings. After Laird's statement to Medicine Calf, "the Indians indulged in a general hearty laugh at this proposition," not at the chief's suggestion. In other words, the Indians were laughing at Morris and not Medicine Calf. The treaty minutes were printed in the *Manitoba Daily Free Press* (Winnipeg), November 8, 1877.

[9] Information provided by Dr. John Laurie, December 15, 1957. This rumor was current among Stony Indians at the treaty council.

stand and threatening to go alone and accept the treaty. While he received no support from the other chiefs, a great number of people agreed with him. These were the ones who, living for the present, saw only the piles of gifts waiting to be distributed. They had no thoughts for the future.

The first break in the deadlock came late Friday night with the heartening news that the main part of the Blood tribe was on its way in. A few hours after dark, the first members of this great tribe followed the trail into the valley, and new tipis soon were pitched beside ones already there. The Bloods, who once had called Crowfoot their own, had arrived with Red Crow at their head. Behind him were the prominent men of the tribe— One Spot, The Moon, and others—while a few hours behind was the aged war chief, Bad Head, with the remainder of the tribe.

A new atmosphere pervaded the camp. The songs took on a new gaiety; old friends were welcomed; and the chiefs were happy that at last the whole nation was together and could reach a final decision.

A council was held far into the night between Red Crow and Crowfoot, brothers-in-law and fellow chieftains. Between them they controlled almost five thousand people and, with the aid of their war chiefs, could turn a thousand warriors into battle.

There is no record of what went on that night. Doubtlessly the Blackfoot chief told of the queen's offer, the negotiations, and the feelings of his tribe. Red Crow, in turn, listened, asked questions, and carefully considered every clause of the proposed treaty. By morning, just as Bad Head was bringing the remainder of the Bloods into camp, Red Crow left Crowfoot's lodge. Immediately he called a council of his chiefs and told them of the proposals.

During this time Crowfoot visited an old medicine man

named Pemmican whose advice he respected. This man was known for his great wisdom and supernatural insight into the problems of the Blackfeet. His advice was constantly sought, but because he was so old he seldom spoke to anyone who came to his lodge. On two occasions when Crowfoot had gone to him about the treaty, he would not answer, but on the third visit he spoke feebly though clearly to his chief.

> I want to hold you back because I am at the edge of a bank. My life is at its end. I hold you back because your life henceforth will be different from what it has been. Buffalo makes your body strong. What you will eat from this money will have your people buried all over these hills. You will be tied down, you will not wander the plains; the whites will take your land and fill it. You won't have your own free will; the whites will lead you by a halter. That is why I say don't sign. But my life is old, so sign if you want to. Go ahead and make the treaty.[10]

Crowfoot was disturbed by his words, which proved to be prophetic; in that very year he was treated by a white doctor for the first time.

Later that morning, Red Crow returned to Crowfoot with the decision of the Bloods. While some of the war chiefs, notably Medicine Calf, Many Spotted Horses, and White Calf, were opposed to the treaty, Red Crow was inclined to favor the terms and had gained the approval of his council. The Bloods would sign if Crowfoot and his followers would agree among themselves to do so. Because he had participated in the negotiations from the beginning, the final word would be left to Crowfoot.

Early that afternoon, October 21, the police cannon again boomed. Slowly the chiefs left their lodges and in small groups they came to the commissioners' tent to take their places on

---

[10] Interview with Many Guns by Hanks, about 1939.

the ground. At a distance, the rest of the nation gathered to watch. Had a decision been reached? There was a hushed expectant silence as Crowfoot arose to speak.

While I speak, be kind and patient. I have to speak for my people, who are numerous, and who rely upon me to follow that course which in the future will tend to their good. The plains are large and wide. We are the children of the plains, it is our home, and the buffalo has been our food always. I hope you look upon the Blackfeet, Bloods and Sarcees as your children now, and that you will be indulgent and charitable to them. They all expect me to speak now for them, and I trust the Great Spirit will put into their breasts to be a good people— into the minds of the men, women and children, and their future generations.

The advice given me and my people has proved to be very good. If the Police had not come to the country, where would we all be now? Bad men and whiskey were killing us so fast that very few, indeed, of us would have been left today. The Police have protected us as the feathers of the bird protect it from the frosts of winter. I wish them all good, and trust that all our hearts will increase in goodness from this time forward. I am satisfied. I will sign the treaty.[11]

The Blackfeet had accepted! And true to their promises, the chiefs from the other tribes announced their willingness to sign. Even Medicine Calf, the Blood war chief, reluctantly agreed. "I must say what all the people say," he conceded, "and I agree with what they say. I cannot make new laws. I will sign."[12]

One by one the head chiefs of each tribe arose and agreed with the Blackfoot leader. Many of them, even Crowfoot himself, may have had some doubts about the treaty, but the treat-

[11] Morris, *Treaties*, 272.
[12] *Ibid.*, 273.

ment accorded them by the Mounted Police had been the main reason for signing. Had their administration not been so fair and their leader not a man of Colonel Macleod's stature, the war chiefs may have overridden the other peaceful chiefs.

After the speeches, Commissioner Laird expressed his pleasure with their decision and told them that the treaty would be prepared for signing on the following day. In the meantime Colonel Macleod would visit with the head chiefs of each tribe to discuss the locations of their new reserves.

A piece of land with five people per square mile as stated in the treaty meant nothing to the Blackfeet; they could not visualize their people being fenced into such a small area. They had wandered all their lives, as had their fathers and grandfathers before them.

If anyone realized the meaning of a reserve, it was Crowfoot. That day he had spoken for the Blackfeet, Bloods, North Piegans, and Sarcees and, knowing that the reserves someday would be their permanent homes, he sought to consolidate them. Red Crow was not interested in a reserve; neither was Bull Head of the Sarcees. Only Eagle Tail of the North Piegans had a preference for the area on the Oldman River near the Porcupine Hills.

Seizing upon the opportunity, Crowfoot suggested a common reserve for the Blackfeet, Bloods, and Sarcees. There was no objection, so he requested Colonel Macleod to set aside land near Blackfoot Crossing and east into the buffalo country. The choice was a narrow piece of land, four miles wide, starting from a point twenty miles upstream from Blackfoot Crossing and extending for about two hundred miles down the river to its confluence with the Red Deer. It passed through some of the best game country but poorest farming land on the prairies. Obviously, hunting rights were uppermost in the minds of Crowfoot and the commissioners in selecting the site.

In addition, a similar plot of land on the south side of the river was set aside for ten years, to prevent traders from camping too close to the Indians and to stop mixed-blood hunters from using campsites along the stream.

On Saturday, September 22, the chiefs gathered to sign the treaty. Each chief was asked to name the men whom he considered his minor chiefs. When the list was complete, Crowfoot's name was placed at the head of the list and he was asked to come forward and sign. Standing before the assembly, Crowfoot pleaded with the commissioners not to deceive him.

> Great Father! Take pity on me with regard to my country, with regard to the mountains, the hills and the valleys; with regard to the prairies, the forests and the waters; with regard to all the animals that inhabit them, and do not take them from myself and my children for ever.[13]

His name was written in English and Blackfoot, and Crowfoot was asked to touch the pen so that his X could be marked. Suspiciously, he asked the reason for this. He was told that the Indian hands, unaccustomed to holding pens, could not mark a proper X, so it was customary for the chief to touch the pen, indicating his willingness to sign. Crowfoot made a motion toward the pen and his mark was inscribed.

Crowfoot had signed the treaty—or had he? As much as he understood the white man's ways, he still was suspicious of any supernatural act which might place him in another man's power, so his hand purposely failed to touch the pen. "Ah," said Crowfoot to a companion after the signing, "I did not touch it."[14]

The question arose at that time and has been repeated many

[13] Father C. Scollen to Lieutenant Colonel A. G. Irvine, April 13, 1879, No. 14924 in the Indian Affairs Archives, Ottawa. Both men had been present at the treaty signing.
[14] *Ibid.*

times since: did the Blackfeet understand the treaty? The old Indians say no. They say their people could not comprehend surrendering the things which were around them. To give up the land was akin to giving up the sky, the mountains, or the buffalo. Father Scollen, who attended the treaty council, voiced the same opinion two years later when writing to Colonel A. G. Irvine, a policeman who also had been there.

> Did these Indians, or do they now, understand the real nature of the treaty made between the Government and themselves in 1877? My answer to this question is unhesitatingly negative....
>
> It may be asked: if the Indians did not understand what the treaty meant, why did they sign it? Because previous to the treaty they had always been kindly dealt with by the Authorities, and did not wish to offend them; and although they had many doubts in their mind as to the meaning of the treaty, yet with this precedent before them, they hoped that it simply meant to furnish them plenty of food and clothing, and particularly the former, every time they stood in need of them....
>
> Crowfoot, who, beyond a doubt, is considered the leading Chief of the Plains, did seem to have a faint notion of the meaning of the treaty. . . . All the other Chiefs followed Crowfoot, and the substance of their speeches was that they agreed with him in all he had said. . . .[15]

Scollen's reasons given for the lack of comprehension were much the same as those given later by the Indians from that era. The interpreters were incapable of explaining the terms of the treaty and could not deal with such matters as land surrenders and reserves. At the same time, how could any interpreter explain to a nomadic Indian that 128 acres of the prairie would be his?

Only Crowfoot understood the treaty in his own way. To him, it simply was a pact of faith between the Indian and the

[15] *Ibid.*

white man. The buffalo were disappearing and the settlers were coming in; nothing could stop them. But the Mounted Police had proven to be honorable representatives of the queen, and now the treaty would give the Blackfeet all the protection and help they would need for years to come.

CHAPTER TEN

STARVATION

The year of the mild winter, *Itsa-estoyi*. That was how the Blackfeet remembered the season of 1877–78. The ground was bare of snow for most of the winter and the weather was unusually mild. But this condition, although pleasant, brought only trouble to the Blackfeet. After the treaty council they had drifted into their winter camps and waited for the snows to drive the buffalo herds toward the foothills. But, instead of snow, prairie fires roared across the land, leaving behind a black barren waste. And the buffalo, finding no feed, remained north and east of the Cypress Hills.

When the Blackfeet realized their predicament, many of them already were starving. Camps were struck and they set out over the blackened plains in search of the shaggy beasts; they were almost to the eastern limits of their hunting grounds before they found them. There, dangerously close to the Crees, Assiniboins, and refugee Sioux, they camped for their winter hunt.

Some time during the winter, Crowfoot received another friendly visit from Sitting Bull. The same words of peace were uttered and Crowfoot accepted them, but now that there was starvation in the camps he advised the Sioux chieftain to keep his people away from the Blackfeet. They had no desire to compete for food with their onetime enemies.[1]

By the spring of 1878, Crowfoot had led his camp, consisting of almost the whole Blackfoot tribe of some two thousand persons, to the western edge of the Great Sand Hills, north of

[1] *Sessional Papers of Canada*, 1879, No. 52, 20.

the Cypress Hills. Nearby were the Bloods under Red Crow and Hind Bull, while a short distance south were the Crees and Assiniboins. At the eastern edge of the same hills was Sitting Bull, with his Sioux camps spread out all the way south to the International Boundary.[2]

A few minor skirmishes took place during that time, but the chiefs were able to keep control. On only one occasion early in May did serious trouble almost arise, when Sitting Bull sent a peace offering of tobacco to the intractable Blood tribe. Instead of cementing relations, the act raised a storm of indignation among the young warriors.

Crowfoot, who was camped in the area, heard of the trouble and rode over to the Blood camp. He found Medicine Calf, the war chief who had opposed the commissioners at the treaty, energetically arguing with his young braves. These men, anxious for war, had organized a party and were trying to leave camp to give Sitting Bull a personal reply to his peace offering. Medicine Calf was trying to stop them when Crowfoot interceded and supported him. After considerable persuasion, the two chiefs were able to talk them out of their dangerous venture. The young braves were convinced that the need for food was greater than the need for glory.

As the spring passed, a new carpet of green grass covered the charred Blackfoot hunting grounds and the dwindling herds returned. Although a few years earlier the country had been black with buffalo, they now were found only in scattered bunches. There still were enough for the Blackfeet, but, with the other tribes invading their land, the daily toll was tremendous.

By summer, Crowfoot was back at Blackfoot Crossing for the annual Sun Dance. There was plenty of meat in the camp, but the chief realized the great days of glory were almost over.

[2] *Fort Benton Record*, April 5, 1878.

The treaty commissioners had said the buffalo would last another ten years, but now, less than a year later, the end was already in sight. He was therefore in a dark mood when Inspector Denny rode into the camp. When he entered Crowfoot's lodge, the policeman realized his news would do nothing to improve the chief's disposition. He explained that the annual treaty payments would soon be made and that the Bloods would be paid separately from the Blackfeet. Red Crow, he said, had considered the question of a reserve and had now decided his tribe should live farther south. Colonel Macleod had agreed, and a reserve would be surveyed along the Belly River.

Crowfoot was dumbfounded. The alliance of the Blackfoot tribes was over before it had begun. His aspirations of leading the united tribes so they could deal with the whites from a position of strength were shattered, with the help and approval of his friend Macleod. In a violent rage, the chief refused to sanction the new agreement, and for the next two days he would not discuss the subject. Then, after a final explosive meeting, he sent Denny from his camp with messages to Colonel Macleod.[3]

A few weeks later, when Macleod and his escort arrived at Blackfoot Crossing to make treaty payments, they found Crowfoot's attitude had not changed. When the payments started, the chief made a long angry speech, accusing the colonel of causing the split between the Bloods and Blackfeet. He claimed also that the police were letting the Sioux come into their hunting grounds, which they never had done before, and were taking advantage of the newly signed treaty. Finally, he demanded that the amount of the treaty payments be the same as the bonus payment given the previous year, twelve dollars a person instead of the agreed five.

[3] Cecil E. Denny, *The Law Marches West*, 112–13.

Some of the Blackfeet were embarrassed by Crowfoot's violent outburst, but the police officer was familiar with the chief's temper. Also, Macleod may have realized the implications of separating the Blackfoot-speaking tribes, for if they were united they were a military threat as well as a political power. Early next morning, as the police were leaving, Crowfoot apologized to Colonel Macleod for the outburst but remained firm in his conviction that the nation had been weakened by the split. While no doubt he would have been flattered to have continued in the role of chief of the entire nation, his reason for wanting the alliance was a more practical one. He knew that the white people were arriving in ever-increasing numbers and soon the Blackfeet would be in the minority. If the Blackfeet stayed together, their voices would continue to be heard and their just demands would receive action. But when separated they lost the bargaining power that a thousand warriors and a huge reserve could give them. However, Crowfoot's fellow chiefs, lacking his foresight, could see only the immediate problems and the needs of their own tribes.

By early winter of 1878–79 not enough meat could be found in the area to feed the Blackfoot camps. A few hunters went south and joined the Bloods, who were following the herds into Montana, while Three Bulls's band went with the Sarcees to search the northeastern prairies in the Neutral Hills. Those who stayed with Crowfoot suffered a severe winter, with heavy snows and little food. On the few occasions when buffalo were found, they were in small wild herds which had been so harassed by hunters that they stampeded at the first suspicion of danger. In desperation the Blackfeet turned to antelope, deer, and elk for food.

By spring, many of the Blackfeet were starving. As the snows turned soft and trickled away into the valleys, Crowfoot's people began to hunt new food on the prairies. Rabbits, gophers, mice, moles, porcupines, badgers—anything with meat on its bones was eaten, no matter how rank. It was not uncommon that spring to see a once-proud warrior stretched out on the prairie holding a noose over the mouth of a gopher hole.

In desperation, Crowfoot sent Three Bulls and some Sarcees to seek the Indian commissioner in Battleford, the territorial capital. They brought their plight before him, telling of the starvation among their people, and asked for help, but without success.

By the summer of 1879, most members of the Bloods and Piegans had followed the herds into Montana. Only Crowfoot remained behind with most of his tribe. From his camp at Blackfoot Crossing he sent hunting parties out to search for game, but they seldom had any success. Gradually, the number of dogs in camp was reduced; although the Blackfeet scorned dog flesh, starvation had left them no choice. After the dogs were gone, parfleche bags, moccasins, and pieces of rawhide were boiled in water to bring out any nourishment they might contain.

The situation was further complicated in summer when a band of almost a thousand destitute Crees arrived at the Crossing and pitched their lodges just three miles away. Perhaps, seeing the Blackfeet at the scene, they thought there was good hunting. They soon learned the truth, but did not leave. The presence of the Crees angered the starving Blackfeet. Their one-time enemies now had the audacity to camp in the heart of the Blackfoot domain and share the scant game that remained. Not until a hotheaded young warrior killed a Cree did the enemy tribe depart.

In mid-July, the newly appointed Indian commissioner, Edgar Dewdney, responded to Three Bulls's pleas and arrived at Blackfoot Crossing. With him he brought flour, tea, and beef as a temporary relief for the camps. Dewdney reported:

On arriving there, I found about 1,300 Indians in a very destitute condition, and many on the verge of starvation. Young
men who were known to be stout and hearty fellows some six
months ago were quite emaciated and so weak they could
hardly work; the old people and widows, who, with their children live on the charity of the younger and more prosperous,
had nothing, and many a pitiable tale was told of the misery
they had endured.[4]

By September these food supplies were gone, and the Blackfeet were beginning to starve again when Commissioner
Dewdney and Colonel Macleod arrived to pay treaty. The
commissioner reported to Crowfoot that many buffalo had
been seen near the Cypress Hills, at the eastern edge of Blackfoot country, so the government had brought supplies for the
tribe to travel to the buffalo. At the same time, the empty
supply wagons could carry the old and crippled back to Fort
Macleod, where the police would care for them.

The day after the Blackfeet received their money, three
days' rations were issued and the camp moved southwest
toward Cypress Hills. At the mouth of the Little Bow River,
Crowfoot met his foster brother Three Bulls, who brought the
disturbing news that the buffalo again were on the move. During the summer, his band had found small herds of twenty or

[4] Report of Edgar Dewdney to the superintendent general of Indian affairs, Ottawa, January 2, 1880, in *Sessional Papers of Canada*, 1880, No. 46,
78. Edgar Dewdney was born in Devonshire, England, in 1835 and went to
British Columbia as a surveyor at the age of twenty-four. After serving as a
Conservative member in the provincial legislature, he was elected to the Canadian House of Commons in 1872. He was appointed Indian commissioner
for the North West Territories in 1879 and assumed the additional position
of lieutenant governor in 1881. He returned to the House of Commons as
member for East Assiniboia in 1888 and was appointed minister of the interior
and superintendent general of Indian affairs. He retired in 1892 to become
lieutenant governor of British Columbia and died in Victoria on August 8,
1916. Although much of his political career was marked with controversy, his
relations with the Indians were good.

thirty animals and had lived quite comfortably. But a few weeks earlier, a large number of prairie fires had started simultaneously in a long line just south of the border and had burned over the vast expanse of country to the Cypress Hills and beyond. The Indians had no doubt that American hide hunters had started the fires to prevent the main herds from returning to Canada. The buffalo now were trapped in a large area from the Little Rockies to the Judith Basin in central Montana.

Traveling eastward across the fire-blackened prairie, the Blackfeet did not find any buffalo until they were almost to the Cypress Hills. There, in a strip which had been missed by the fire, they located a few scattered herds still on Canadian soil. But before the end of the year, almost all these buffalo had been killed. Crowfoot had never taken his people into American territory before, but less than fifty miles away was the International Boundary and beyond it were more buffalo. Reluctantly he turned south and late in 1879 he led the Blackfeet into the land of the Long Knives.

LAND OF THE LONG KNIVES

Crow-Foot has always been the leader of noted murderers, and is responsible for the death of more than one emigrant and prospector, yet this red butcher has been the pet of the Mounted Police ever since the latter arrived in the country.[1]

On this note the Montana press welcomed Crowfoot to its territory. The reception was neither unexpected nor unjustified, for the Montana ranching industry had been thriving for several years with little trouble from the local Indians. But the trapping of the last buffalo herd in the Judith Basin area had brought thousands of native hunters from all parts of the plains. The settlers saw some justification for the presence of American Indians, whom the army could shepherd back to their reservations. But the Canadian Indians were another problem, for the ranchers felt the queen's government was encouraging them to go to Montana to save the expense of feeding them. They were right too, for Indian Commissioner Dewdney's meeting with the Blackfeet in the autumn of 1879 had been designed for just that purpose, as he admitted in a private letter.

I advised them strongly to go and gave them some provisions to take them off. They continued to follow the Buffalo further and further south until they reached the main herd and there they remained. . . . I consider their remaining away saved the Govt. $100,000 at least.[2]

---

[1] Fort Benton Record, December 12, 1879.
[2] Edgar Dewdney to D. L. McPherson, August 4, 1881, in the Macdonald Papers, Vol. 210, 242–43.

There was little the United States Army could do. Attempts were made to escort the Bloods and other tribes to the International Boundary line, but once in Canada there was no further restraint and soon they were back with the buffalo. By winter, northeastern Montana was crowded with Bloods, Blackfeet, Crees, Sarcees, Assiniboins, Sioux, Gros Ventres, Crows, Piegans, and mixed-bloods. Stockmen feared cattle killing; settlers feared an uprising.

Crowfoot's tribe wandered south about fifty miles into Montana and made its first winter camp on the Milk River near the Bear Paw Mountains. Later, when they drifted south to the Missouri River, the Blackfeet found plenty of buffalo and remained there for the rest of the winter.

Their adopted hunting grounds were along the north side of the river from the Bear Paw Mountains to the Little Rockies. The main buffalo herd was farther south, but there was enough food for the whole tribe north of the river. Most of the other tribes were in the wide Judith Basin, with Big Bear's Crees being closest to Crowfoot's camp. The Sioux, still exiled in Canada, made frequent trips into the district but hurried back whenever the blue-coated army patrols appeared.

Soon after the Blackfeet had camped on the river, the tragic days of the past were brought vividly back to them. For five years the taste of whisky had been almost unknown to the tribe. In the queen's domain the Mounted Police had wiped out the liquor trade and all the evils that went with it. But in Montana Crowfoot found the old conditions still existed. As soon as there were meat and buffalo robes in the camp, the ragged traders with wagons of whisky appeared on the scene. Drunken orgies, fights, and killings followed. Just when the Blackfeet needed hides to replace their worn lodges and to make new clothing, the irresistible firewater was poured into their camps.

Crowfoot saw the familiar faces of men who had visited

their camps in the old days, and there were new men who followed the hunters like the gray wolves after the buffalo herds. But all had the same purpose, to get buffalo robes as cheaply as possible. False bottoms in tin cups, laudanum in the whisky, or any other means were used to this end.

In one incident, after the tribe had lost a number of horses, the Indians insisted on exchanging robes for any surplus animals of the traders. The American freebooters made the trade and, as a sign of generosity, provided the camp with free whisky. That same evening, while everyone was drunk, they stole the horses back from the Indians and left them afoot and destitute.[3]

Crowfoot did his best to keep order in his camp, but he missed the support of the Mounted Police. His young warriors openly disobeyed his commands; fights and killings over whisky and women were common; and horse stealing could not be controlled. All Crowfoot could do was to prevent open conflict with the enemy tribes in the area.

On one occasion, a war party of Crees came into the Blackfoot camp at night and stole some of Crowfoot's horses. Several young men immediately volunteered to retaliate, but the chief demurred. He rode alone for several miles along the river looking for the Cree camp but came back empty-handed. He then told two of his young men to go farther afield to see if they could recover the horses. They returned a few days later and reported that the young Cree warriors had refused to give them up, but their chiefs finally had seized the horses and given them to Crowfoot's men.

A short time later, another party of Crees who had been following some Blood hunters accidentally discovered Crowfoot's camp. Waiting until nightfall, they were creeping toward the horse herd when they were seen by an observant guard. The

[3] *Sessional Papers of Canada,* 1882, Part I, 39.

boy immediately told Crowfoot, but, when his warriors wanted to ambush the would-be thieves, the chief would not allow it. Instead, he rode out boldly into the darkness and approached the armed raiders. He could have been shot, but either from fear or surprise the Crees did nothing. Crowfoot said he knew why they were hiding but told them the days of fighting and stealing were past. Instead, he invited them to his lodge. The surprised warriors accepted and remained for several days in the chief's lodge, where they were treated as honored guests.[4] "This was one of Crowfoot's hardest deeds," said an old Indian who had witnessed the incident. "It happened at night and no one else would have had the nerve to do this. It was the only time such a thing had been done."[5]

But added to Crowfoot's worries about the social problems of his people was another peril which confronted him that winter. As soon as he had arrived at the Milk River camp, the Bloods and Piegans told him of the strange speeches being made by the mixed-bloods who were visiting their camps. These people, some of whom were wintering in the area, had a new leader, a man named Louis Riel.

The name was not known to Crowfoot but was famous throughout much of Canada. In 1869, when negotiations were under way to transfer the West from Great Britain to Canada, Riel had rallied the mixed-bloods of Red River Settlement to oppose the move. He rightfully believed that the residents in the West should have some part in the transactions and feared that his people would lose the rights to their small farms. His worst suspicions were confirmed when Canada sent surveyors and administrators to the area before the transfer was official. Riel then led his mixed-bloods in open rebellion, capturing Fort Garry and arresting those who sided with the Canadian gov-

4 Interview with Duck Chief by Hanks, about 1939.
5 *Ibid.*

ernment. Later, after Riel had executed one of the prisoners, a military force was sent out from Canada to put down the revolt. Riel was forced to flee to the United States but continued to press for mixed-blood rights.

As a result of Riel's efforts, the province of Manitoba was formed around the Red River Settlement, and mixed-blood rights were recognized. A grateful people elected him as their member of the Canadian Parliament for two terms, but he never held office, as he was still a fugitive.

In 1877 and 1878, Riel had been committed to mental institutions in eastern Canada, but on his release he had moved west and by the autumn of 1879 was traveling with mixed-blood hunters in the Montana area.

Two days after the Blackfeet had set up camp, Riel and four counselors came to see Crowfoot. Riel was thirty-five years old and Crowfoot was fifty when the two men met. A Missouri River trader described Riel:

> He was a fine-looking man, even if his bright eyes were a bit shifty . . . and he had such courtly manners. When still thirty or forty yards away he would remove his wide sombrero with a grand sweep and approach you bowing and smiling, and filling the air with high-flown compliments.[6]

Riel's talk with Crowfoot was a long one and a surprising one for the Blackfoot chief. Riel said that the buffalo had left their territory because of the presence of the Mounted Police, that the Canadian government was not going to look after the Blackfeet, and that the treaty would be ignored and forgotten. He said that the mixed-bloods wanted to help them and that a great council of all the Indians and mixed-bloods would be held in the spring.[7] According to Crowfoot:

[6] James Willard Schultz, *My Life as an Indian*, 186.
[7] Jean L'Heureux to Edgar Dewdney, September 24, 1880, No. 34527 in the Indian Affairs Archives.

He wanted me to join with all the Sioux, and the Crees, and half-breeds. The idea was to have a general uprising and capture the North-West, and hold it for the Indian race and the Métis [mixed-bloods]. We were to meet at Tiger Hills, in Montana; we were to have a government of our own. I refused, but the others were willing. . . ."[8]

Riel's words were eloquent, but to Crowfoot they still advocated a disastrous war with the whites. The phrasing was far different from the message he had received from Sitting Bull in 1876, and the motives of the two men could not be compared. But war was war, whether for extermination or self-government, and Crowfoot was convinced his people could never win. Besides, his faith in the Mounted Police was strong and he hoped that the problems of the Blackfeet could be solved by peaceful means.

After the meeting, Riel invited Crowfoot's renegade interpreter, Jean L'Heureux, to a meeting at the cabin of Trottier, one of the mixed-blood counselors, who lived about fifteen miles from the Blackfoot camp. L'Heureux later described the meeting in a letter to the prime minister.

I soon learned the whole plan of the affair, which was nothing less than the invasion and taking possession of the North-West Territories, with the help of a general uprising of all the Indian tribes, united to the Half-breeds. . . . That R . . .[9] was to be Governor, and Riel the first Minister of his

[8] John Maclean, *Canadian Savage Folk*, 380.
[9] L'Heureux's letter in the Macdonald Papers is a copy and the name is shown as an "R" followed by four periods. He likely was referring to Joseph Royal, who was the Conservative member for Provencher at the time. He had gone to Manitoba as a lawyer in 1871 and had assisted in the defense in the cases of *Queen* v. *Ambroise Lépine* and *Queen* v. *André Nault*, arising from the murder of Thomas Scott in the rebellion of 1869–70. He also was a prominent journalist, who founded *Le Métis* in Winnipeg. He served in the Manitoba legislature from 1870 to 1879, holding the portfolios of provincial secretary, public works, and attorney general. He was elected to the House of

cabinet, where a seat was to be given to the Indian Chief who, with his people, would help the Half-breeds most in the contemplated invasion. . . .

The practical plan was to take opportunity of some horse difficulties of the Police with the Half-breeds; attack and take possession of Wood Mountain Fort; they were then to make for Fort Walsh, and from the last place, make for Battleford. The Blackfeet were to take possession of Macleod. After that last exploit, Riel was to proclaim a provisional Government. . . . A general meeting was appointed for all the tribes at Tiger Hills, on Milk River, for the last week of May [1880], and from there the order to march was to be issued in the beginning of June.[10]

L'Heureux was asked to join the mixed-bloods and to induce the chiefs to unite with Riel. Instead, the French-Canadian agreed with Crowfoot that the Blackfeet should move south to the Missouri, where they would be away from the mixed-blood influences and where they would find more buffalo. However, the agitators continued to visit the camps of the Blackfeet, Bloods, Crees, and other tribes during the winter. At these meetings, prominent chiefs listened to the orations of Riel and his men. Riel told them of his capture of Fort Garry and of the important men in eastern Canada who would support him in his plans. On one occasion, he took the treaty parchment from Little Pine, a Cree chief, hurled it to the ground, and trampled it. This treaty, he said, was no good and he would give them a better one when the new republic was formed.[11]

But the words of this self-appointed savior had little effect on Crowfoot. While Little Pine and others may have been in-

Commons in 1879 and remained until 1888, when he was appointed lieutenant governor of the North West Territories. There is no indication that Royal was aware of Riel's plans for him in his proposed invasion.

[10] L'Heureux to Macdonald, November 1, 1886, in the Macdonald Papers.
[11] *Ibid.* Also Maclean, *op. cit.*, 380.

terested in these dreams of a native empire, Crowfoot's mind followed another path. He had no wish to join a revolution which would destroy all that he had so painstakingly tried to build.

During this time, Riel also tried to get guns and ammunition for his cause. A wagon train en route to Fort Ellis, Montana, with ten cases of guns and a supply of ammunition was stopped by a mixed-blood party. Riel offered the drivers double their usual fee, a thousand-dollar bonus, and their freighters' bond if they would leave the wagons unguarded for a time. When they refused, Riel doubled his offer and warned them his men could seize the wagons. However, the freighters were not to be coerced into changing their minds, so Riel finally let them go.[12]

As spring approached, the American authorities were told of the proposed gathering at Tiger Hills. A body of troops was sent to the area, and the Indians were told that anyone congregating there would be sent back to Canada under guard. With the plan thwarted while still in its embryo stage, Riel gave up his invasion plans and, with about two hundred families, moved south to the Judith Basin.[13]

[12] Joseph Kinsey Howard, Strange Empire, a Narrative of the Northwest, 340. This information was given to Howard by Frank P. Eckley, a freighter in the party.

[13] Much of the information about this episode was provided by L'Heureux in letters to Macdonald, September 24, 1880, and November 1, 1886. His statements were supported by Crowfoot in an interview with G. H. Ham, Toronto Mail, January 26, 1886. When the information first was passed on to Dewdney and the prime minister, Assistant Indian Commissioner E. T. Galt was asked to investigate. On March 20, 1880, he wired Dewdney from Helena, Montana, "Telegram received, have seen General Rugher [Colonel Thomas R. Rugher], writing fully about L'Heureux matter, nothing in it." But on September 4, 1884, Assistant Indian Commissioner Hayter Reed wrote to Dewdney, "Possibly the fact may have been known to the Department before, but I have discovered, and on undoubted authority, that Riel while on the other side of the line was endeavoring to incite our Indians to rebellion; this was at the time the Buffalo were south & Big Bear and others followed them." In the Macdonald Papers, North-West Rebellion, Vol. 4, 123.

In the meantime, the Blackfeet continued to hunt north of the Missouri but found the buffalo becoming scarce again. Not only were they being reduced in numbers, but the disorganized Sioux hunts had frightened many of the animals across the river. During the summer, Sitting Bull paid another visit to Crowfoot. The Sioux chief explained that his people had to stay in the Cypress Hills but came south to hunt. He wanted peace between the two tribes so that his men could get meat for the camps. "We will be friends to the end of our lives," said Sitting Bull. "My children will be your children and yours mine. From now on we will never fight again and we will be on the same side at all times."[14] He then told how he had named his eight-year-old favorite son Crowfoot, in honor of the Blackfoot chief.

Crowfoot was pleased and agreed to the continued peace. He invited the Sioux to join the Blackfeet in a dance and, later, a feast in his lodge. The promise was repeated that peace forever would prevail between the Sioux and Blackfeet. A few days later, a war party of Sioux raided the Blackfoot camp and ran off a large herd of horses. Crowfoot was furious at this breach of treaty and publicly denounced Sitting Bull as a fork-tongued liar. Henceforth, he said, the Sioux were their enemies and would be treated as such. The two chiefs never met again.

By the autumn of 1880, the buffalo were so scarce north of the Missouri River that Crowfoot realized he would have to move. Hopefully, he sent a messenger to Commissioner Dewdney, asking if his people could go back to Canada to be protected and fed by the Great Mother. Dewdney sent word that "if they were within reach of the buffalo to remain with them as I saw no means of feeding them if they returned. . . . I would

14 G. H. Gooderham, Indian agent, Blackfoot Reserve, to W. S. Campbell (Stanley Vestal), Norman, Oklahoma, September 6, 1930. A copy of this letter is in possession of the author.

123

hold their annuity money for them until they came back. ...."[15]

The only alternative was to move farther south into Montana Territory in search of the main herd. Early in October, the tribe crossed the Missouri and chose a new campsite near a trading post at Fort Carrol. Soon they found that the main herd was moving northward toward them, so unthinkingly they formed a barrier which wiped out any hope that the animals might return to Canada. The Blackfeet soon were joined by Big Bear and his Cree camp and the two tribes lived side by side in harmony throughout the winter. The Bloods, who still were at war with the Crees, went south to the Snowy Mountains, while the Piegans camped farther west.

Late in the fall, another band of wanderers came into the valley. The Blackfeet recognized the screeching Red River carts before any of them came into sight. They knew the Cree mixed-bloods were back among them. They had just finished their summer hunt and had voted to winter at Fort Carrol. So for the remainder of the season Riel, Big Bear, and Crowfoot were camped almost side by side in the same river bottom. There can be little doubt that the three came to know each other well. And again L'Heureux was concerned about the effect of Riel on the Blackfoot chief. He reported to Commissioner Dewdney:

> Riel and his frontier partisans are expected to renew their last year's tactics for fomenting trouble and half-breeding conspiracies with the Indians. He is only waiting at the Judith Basin the result of Miles' campaign against the hostile Sioux, for a political campaign of his own whose program is "That the N.W.T. is the natural property of the Indian and Half-breed, ought to be set apart for their exclusive use, ruled & governed by them alone." That is his modest motto.[16]

[15] Dewdney to McPherson, August 4, 1881, *loc. cit.*
[16] L'Heureux to Dewdney, September 24, 1880. No. 34527 in the Indian Affairs Archives.

But if Crowfoot was subjected to these orations during the winter, he still was not swayed. Both men were leaders, but their ideals were poles apart. One was a believer in peaceful coexistence with the white man, the other a proponent of a self-governing Indian and mixed-blood nation.

That winter was a severe one, with heavy snows blocking the Judith Basin and the temperatures hovering below zero for long periods. The results were hardship and privation for some of the camps, particularly those which had traded their horses and robes for whisky. This caused a further deterioration of camp life as Indians spread out in search of food. There were more drunken fights in the camps, bitter disputes between enemy hunters, and troubles with white ranchers. Cattle killing became common, and the ranchers' anger mounted in the face of apparent inactivity by the army.

About three hundred horses were stolen from the Cree and Blackfoot camps near Fort Carrol during the winter, and about twenty Indians were killed. Another raid on the Blackfoot herd cost the Sioux eight men, although another one hundred and sixty horses were stolen.[17] But the trouble did not always originate with the Indians. Among the Bloods, twenty-six horses were stolen by white men in a raid, and on Arrow Creek the white renegades took another thirty. A Blood was shot by a wood chopper on the Missouri without cause, and at Box Elder white men slept at a Blood camp at night and then ran off all their horses.[18] At the root of much of the trouble was whisky, as the traders constantly were visiting the Indian camps. Then, starving and destitute, the Indians turned to ranchers' cattle for food.

In an attempt to find a solution to their problem, the ranchers called a protest meeting in Fort Benton. Feeling that mili-

17 *Ibid.*
18 Dewdney to Macdonald, October 26, 1881, in the Macdonald Papers.

tary action was not effective, they formed a "citizens' organization for the protection of themselves and stock from the depredations of the Indians . . . and to proceed against the Indians as necessity compels. . . ."[19]

One of the irate ranchers wrote to the United States secretary of the interior:

> . . . since last August, these two counties [Meagher and Choteau] have been overrun with hordes of alien [Canadian] Indians, principally Blackfeet, Bloods, Piegans and Crees, to the number of about 350 lodges. . . . these Indians, ostensibly here for the purpose of hunting buffalo, have killed and eaten many of our cattle, and this, too, in instances where there was an abundance of buffalo within ten miles of their camps. . . .
>
> Some weeks ago these Indians began moving north, and we thought we would have at least a temporary respite from their depredations, but we now hear that Crow Foot's band of 140 lodges of Blackfeet, and some forty or fifty lodges of Crees, have turned back from Carrol, on the Missouri River, saying that they will not return to their own country but will remain here. . . .[20]

The rancher claimed that five per cent of their entire herds had been slaughtered by Indians during the winter, a total of three thousand cattle worth sixty thousand dollars.[21] The anger of the ranchers was so great that many were prepared to take matters into their own hands. The Montana press was filled with letters and editorials saying "that the cattle men are prepared to protect their property by force of arms if other measures fail"[22] and "let us rise up like men and defend our prop-

[19] Benton (Montana) River Press, April 27, 1881.
[20] Granville Stuart to Samuel J. Kirkwood, printed in the Benton River Press, May 4, 1881.
[21] Paul C. Phillips (ed.), Forty Years on the Frontier as Seen in the Journals and Reminiscences of Granville Stuart, 154.
[22] Benton River Press, August 17, 1881.

erty, and teach these breech-clouted pets of the government that we have some rights. . . ."[23] However, the bitter winter passed before the stockmen were organized or realized the true extent of their losses.

Most of the Blackfeet survived the winter, but not without hardship and misery. The camps had become completely demoralized by the rotgut whisky and the lawless white men who hovered nearby. Indians traded their robes and meat for liquor, and, when they had nothing to trade, they turned their wives to prostitution in the white settlements. The young men ignored their chiefs and disobeyed their orders. Even the Black Soldiers, the men's society which was supposed to keep peace and order in the camps, became as wild and uncontrollable as their brothers. Crowfoot found they would not listen to his suggestions but were like a police force which had become corrupt.

With practically no power over his people, Crowfoot could only watch with sadness. He was a powerful chief, but in the face of whisky and lawless white men he could do nothing. And he was not alone, for there was not a chief in all the disorganized camps in Montana who was in actual command of his people.

Besides the Indians who died of starvation and in tribal skirmishes, many perished when an epidemic of measles struck the camp at the onset of winter. In the spring of 1881, there was more mourning when an epidemic of mumps carried off more people. Among those who died was Iron Shield, Crowfoot's only full brother, the boy who had come with him from the Blood camp almost half a century earlier.[24]

By February, 1881, the destruction of the last big buffalo herd was so great that Crowfoot had to lead his people farther

23 *Ibid.*, August 31, 1881.
24 Interview with Mrs. Jennie Duck Chief, March 5, 1957.

south to the Musselshell River. At Fort Carrol, the traders had taken in four thousand buffalo robes, while itinerant whisky peddlers had acquired an even larger number. The total take during the season was so large that there could be no doubt the buffalo were almost wiped out.

Traveling along the Musselshell, the Blackfeet did not find the main buffalo herd. The Judith Basin was almost devoid of game and any large bands of buffalo which had survived the winter had fled southeast, or north to the Cypress Hills area. Realizing they could no longer hunt as a tribe, Crowfoot advised his minor chiefs to take their people in separate bands in hope of finding the isolated herds which remained.

By early May, 1881, about a thousand followers were still with their head chief. Most of the others had drifted north to the Cypress Hills area and, finding nothing, had returned to Canada. When they straggled into Fort Macleod, they were hungry, exhausted, and confused. Where had the buffalo gone? A few years ago the plains were black with them. Now there were none. What had happened? Was it true that the Sun had opened a great hole in the earth and driven his animals into it? These were questions no one could answer. All they knew was that the buffalo were gone. By the end of May, more than five hundred Blackfeet had reached Fort Macleod and were receiving rations.[25] The police wanted them to go on to Blackfoot Crossing, but they refused to move until their chief arrived.

Down on the Musselshell, Crowfoot hated to admit, even to himself, that there were no more buffalo. His camp was reduced to poverty, mostly through the whisky traffic, and most of the horses were gone. Crowfoot still had a few animals, but these were loaned to the weak and helpless for moving

[25] Indian Agent N. T. Macleod to Lieutenant Governor Dewdney, Fort Macleod, June 1, 1881, in the Blood Correspondence, Vol. 1, 89.

camp. Even his best buffalo runners, horses which never had worked except in the hunt, were pressed into service. He knew the need for buffalo runners had suddenly ended.

During May, Father Scollen arrived from Fort Calgary in search of Crowfoot.[26] When he found the pitiful camp, he urged the chief to go back to Canada, where flour and beef were waiting for him. But Crowfoot shook his head. He must stay a little while longer. There were rumors that the Gros Ventres were chasing the buffalo from the southeast toward their camps. There were still a few thousand animals left, and it might be possible to outfit his people for the long journey home. They needed meat for hungry mouths and robes for their worn lodges and clothing.

Each day, hunting parties took the few remaining horses out in search of food. At nightfall they returned, sometimes with meat but usually empty handed.

One day early in June, a hunting party did not return. The Blackfeet were worried that it had met an enemy war party or army patrol and had been wiped out. Others thought the hunters had gone north to join their relatives in Canada. But they were wrong, for a few days later the jubilant hunters rode into camp with seventy head of horses. They had gone on a raiding party against the Crows on the Yellowstone River. Now, they said, the tribe would have enough horses to travel. All year the Crows and other enemies had been robbing the Blackfeet, and at last they had some horses back. There was enough meat in the camp to take them all the way home, now that they did not have to walk.

But their actions had put Crowfoot in a predicament. He knew that the raid had taken place on the Crow Reservation and that the U.S. Cavalry soon would be in pursuit. The resentment of the ranchers had been running high, and trouble

[26] *Benton* (Montana) *Weekly Record,* August 4, 1881.

with the authorities would be a perfect excuse to proclaim the tribe as "hostiles." There were several branded horses in the herd, probably stolen by Crows from the ranchers, but their presence would be proof that his people were raiding the white settlers. It could be enough to cause an attack on the whole camp. On the other hand, almost all their own horses had been stolen or traded for whisky. There was some meat in camp but not enough to take them on foot on a four-hundred-mile journey.

Crowfoot, the peacemaker, did what he thought was best. Choosing his most trusted men to accompany him, he personally took the herd to the army post at Rocky Point.[27] There he learned that several companies of cavalry already were being dispatched from Fort Assiniboine to search for the raiders. The order from General John R. Brooke was "to move those Indians or bury them."[28]

Crowfoot had expected a few more weeks to get provisions, but now, sick at heart, he returned to his camp. He knew that, except for Big Bear and a few Crees, all the other Indians had returned to Canada. If the army was out for blood, they would know where to come. The horse-stealing incident had sealed the Blackfeet's fate. Sadly, Crowfoot ordered his followers to strike camp. They were going to walk back home.

[27] *Ibid.*, September 1, 1881.
[28] *Benton River Press*, April 27, 1881.

CHAPTER TWELVE

THE LONG WALK HOME

Out from the Musselshell and north toward the Missouri the pitiful camp made its way. The Blackfeet packed only their most precious belongings on the few remaining horses and dogs. Skin lodges, horse travois, and other heavy objects were left behind or later abandoned on the trail. Only the very old, the very young, and the crippled were able to ride.

Early in June, the tribe passed through the badlands and crossed the Missouri at Fort Carrol. There, a few more robes were exchanged for food, but again the vulturous whisky traders descended upon them. Many of the Blackfeet, sick at heart, tried to forget their troubles in the poisonous rotgut. There was some singing and dancing in the camp that night, but next morning the warriors awoke to find their grim plight had only become worse.

When they finally pulled away from this last settlement on American soil, they had less meat and fewer horses than before. And, to add to the tragedy, the hunger-weakened children began to show signs of illness. Two of the white man's diseases, measles and scarletina, had joined the caravan.[1] The only healthy ones left in the caravan seemed to be the overworked horses. Yet even these had received the lethal gift of scabby mange before departing from Montana.

So, with hunger, disillusionment, and disease in his camp, Crowfoot led his people along the fringe of the Little Rockies and north past the Bear Paw Mountains. In the hazy mist to the

---

[1] Indian Agent N. T. Macleod to Lieutenant Governor Dewdney, Fort Macleod, June 1, 1881, in the Blood Correspondence, Vol. 1, 89.

131

north were the low green ridges of the Cypress Hills, and Canada. Each day they pushed onward, as fast as tired feet and overburdened horses could walk. Children sickened and died; old people succumbed to starvation and exhaustion; hungry dogs fought among themselves, and the supply of pemmican became smaller and smaller.

One of Crowfoot's biggest problems during the trek was the warrior society, the Black Soldiers. When they wanted to retaliate after their camps were raided, Crowfoot had intervened. When they wanted to travel farther south after the buffalo, Crowfoot had stayed on the Musselshell. Each act of contradiction had made the warriors more angry at what they considered to be inaction in the face of hardship and danger. The final act of returning the stolen Crow horses almost caused the younger warriors and Black Soldiers to revolt. However, when the main party moved northward, the malcontents remained with them. Grumbling and hostile, they were the ones responsible for the whisky traders doing such a good business at Fort Carrol. They were the ones who traded meat and horses, then grumbled again when the hardships increased.

After several days of slow, weary travel, the ragged Blackfoot survivors began to cross the line into Canada. By this time they were spread out in a long irregular line, with the most mobile bands a day or two ahead of the others.

Crowfoot, with all his horses lent to the needy, plodded along near the end of the line. Remembering his generosity in the bountiful years, the old people, widows, and other helpless ones gathered around him to share his scanty food supplies.

At nightfall, the travelers halted wearily on the trail. Hungry and tired, they lay down and slept. By the time the sun was setting, the only sounds were the mournful howling of starving dogs, the wailing of mourning women, and the faltering voices of medicine men dutifully performing their evening rituals.

By the end of June, the starving Indians began straggling into Fort Walsh in the Cypress Hills. There they were told that the Sioux also were hungry and were dangerous. The Mounted Police wanted no trouble between the two tribes, so they shared what little rations they had and advised Crowfoot and his people to move on.

After resting a few days, the Blackfeet set out again. West from the hills they went over the arid plains where, two winters earlier, they had killed many buffalo on their way to Montana. Now, crossing the same flats, all they saw were bleached bones, acres of dung, the winding trails, and dried wallows. All the signs of buffalo were there, but the great monarch was gone.

Occasionally, in the bitter days that followed, the Blackfeet saw small herds of antelope. Sometimes their hunters were successful and for a short time there were a few pounds of fresh meat in the camps. But an antelope carcass did not last long in a camp of a thousand starving Indians. Usually, the meager reserves of pemmican were doled out, a tiny morsel having to last all day. But even with this rigid rationing, the food supplies were gone long before they reached Fort Macleod. The daily trek had slowed to a few miles; the young men as well as the old were unable to keep up a steady pace. There were frequent rests, but even this slow pace was too much for the starving people. Each day, new voices wailed the Death Songs as the spirits of their loved ones departed for the Sand Hills. The wooded coulees and the bare hilltops along the route were dotted with the graves of those who died. Finally, after almost six weeks of walking and starving, the Blackfeet at last saw the palisaded walls of Fort Macleod. And there, camped along the river bottom, was the remainder of the tribe still waiting for their chief.

Crow Foot arrived here on the 20th ulto with 1,064 followers, all in a most destitute condition. A large proportion of his
followers consisted of old men, women and children. They
were nearly all on foot.[2]

Crowfoot saw at once that nothing was the same in his old
land. The formerly neat lodges of the Blackfeet were ragged
and torn, the once-gallant warriors were subdued, and even
the children had lost the spark of life. The buffalo were gone,
the old life was gone. Scores of fresh graves dotted the countryside from the Oldman River to the Missouri. Warriors who
had defeated every enemy in battle were reduced to bony
derelicts before starvation and disease carried the life from
their bodies. No one knows exactly how many people from the
Blackfoot tribe died during those starvation years, but from
1879 to 1881 at least one thousand members of the nation in
Canada perished.

This was a tremendous loss, and as Crowfoot led his pitiful
following on the last hundred-mile leg of their journey to
Blackfoot Crossing, he knew that their days of traveling were
over. No more would they wander across the grassy plains.
Gone was the excitement of trading with the white men on
the Saskatchewan, or driving the buffalo over cliffs to get
a winter's supply of meat. No more could a scout stand on a
bald hillock, watching the orderly procession of horses, travois,
dogs, and people as they moved in safety under his protective eye.

These things were gone, and what remained? A small plot
of land in the middle of their domain. Here they would camp
in the river bottoms and receive the beef and flour of the white
men. They would scratch the earth and grow turnips and other
vegetables. The Blackfeet, the Real People, had lost the shaggy
beast which provided Real Meat, and in doing so they had lost

[2] *Ibid.*, August 4, 1881, Vol. 1, 95.

their freedom. Many of the old people believed that soon the Blackfeet would follow the buffalo into oblivion.

The days and weeks that followed did nothing to raise the spirits of the dejected tribe. They found the country completely devoid of game and waited patiently in the daily line-ups for beef and flour. The Indian Department employees, many of whom were rough frontiersmen, showed little respect for the poverty-stricken people. They often were rude and belligerent, even to the chiefs, and treated the Blackfeet as though they were little better than the dirt under their feet. The warriors also looked on helplessly while their women turned to prostitution to obtain extra rations.

Another basis for complaint were the rations themselves, which at that time consisted of a pound of beef and half a pound of flour a day per person. The flour often was spoiled and even the regular issue was an inferior grade which could find a market only at the Indian Agency.[3] The beef, while of a better quality, did not compare with the buffalo meat. To the Blackfeet, it tasted sickly sweet and did not have the nourishment of Real Food. In addition, the contractors were allowed to keep the heads and offal and caused resentment by selling these pieces to the highest bidder. The Blackfeet, who knew that the cattle were being bought with Indian Department money, did not feel they should pay extra for any particular parts of the animals. But who would listen? Even Crowfoot's old friend, Colonel Macleod, could no longer help, for he had retired from the Mounted Police to become a district magistrate.

But Crowfoot still was glad to be back in his own land. The familiar hills bordering Blackfoot Crossing had regained their

---

[3] The flour issued to the Blackfeet when they first returned to Canada was described by an inspector as "not quite unfit for food." (T. P. Wadsworth to Dewdney, July 5, 1881, No. 29506 in the Indian Affairs Archives.)

luxuriant grass after the devastating prairie fires, and any horses which had not died in the mange epidemic were turned out to graze. The whisky traders who had done so much harm had been miraculously halted at the invisible line between the lands of the Long Knives and the Red Coats.

In September, about five weeks after their return, a messenger from Fort Calgary brought word to Crowfoot that Commissioner Dewdney was on his way from Battleford and was bringing with him the son-in-law of the queen. A few days later a long procession of wagons and horses followed the trail down the slopes to the camp of more than two hundred Blackfoot lodges. Crowfoot, tired and sick from his grueling ordeals, leaned heavily upon a staff as he watched the men approach. He saw Dewdney and the young man who was the son-in-law of the Great Mother. Then Crowfoot's face brightened with a happy smile as he recognized the guide of the party, Poundmaker, his adopted son. It had been several years since they had been together, and he saw with pride that his son had become a handsome and dignified warrior.

A tent was pitched and a request was sent out for the chiefs to meet the Marquis of Lorne, governor general of Canada and son-in-law of Queen Victoria. First came Indians in battle array astride their skinny cayuses, galloping forward and firing their rifles into the air. Behind them came the women and children, who gathered respectfully in the distance. When all were present the chiefs, each carrying a Union Jack, came forward to shake hands with Commissioner Dewdney and Lord Lorne. First came Crowfoot, followed by Old Sun, Heavy Shield, and Bull Head, chief of the Sarcees. After smoking the traditional pipe, each chief arose and delivered a message to Lord Lorne, with Poundmaker interpreting. They spoke of losing their lands to the white man, the disappearance of the buffalo, and the increasing numbers of white men who were moving in. They spoke of the small rations and the poor flour, and they asked for more help.[4]

Crowfoot was the last to speak. He arose, grasped the hand of Lord Lorne, and offered him one of his few remaining horses as a gift. He then made an impassioned plea for more rations for his destitute people and more help to make them self-sufficient. Standing in his tattered robes, Crowfoot presented himself unashamedly as a destitute spokesman for his starving people. The Reverend James MacGregor, a member of the party, wrote:

> I have rarely seen a more touching sight than the poor infirm chief, with his finely chissled countenance and bright smile, as, leaning heavily on his staff, and worse clad than any of his followers, he moved forward to his place; the shabby clothes, which the poorest artisan would be ashamed to wear, contrasted sadly with the Victoria medal which he wore on his breast.[5]

Responding to Crowfoot's plea, Lord Lorne advised him to lead his people in breaking the land and turning to agriculture as a livelihood. He told him that the old days were gone and the Blackfeet could no longer wander in search of the buffalo. "I shall take your advice," replied Crowfoot. "I have been first in fighting; I shall now be first in working."[6]

As a parting gift, Lord Lorne gave Crowfoot a shotgun, but would not take the chief's horse from the destitute tribe.

When the vice-regal party left, life resumed its normal pace, although Poundmaker brightened Crowfoot's life by remaining in his lodge for several days. The Cree had become a chief

[4] Lorne, Marquis of, *Canadian Pictures; Drawn with Pen and Pencil*, 171–72.
[5] MacGregor, Rev. James A., "Lord Lorne in Alberta," *Alberta Historical Review*, Spring, 1964, 7.
[6] *Ibid.*, p. 8.

and had a small group of followers at Battleford. Like his foster father, he was a proponent of peace but a defender of his people's rights. He had learned much from Crowfoot during those early years and was beginning to gain the same reputation and prestige among the Crees that his father held with the Blackfeet. Crowfoot was proud of his adopted son and the bond between them was stronger than any of the chief's with his own children. It was with sadness that he saw the young warrior return north a few weeks later to the land of the Crees.

CHAPTER THIRTEEN

A FAITH DESTROYED

By 1881, settlers on the western prairies still were represented by only a few isolated villages and communities. Far to the east of Blackfoot country, the Red River Settlement had grown into the bustling city of Winnipeg, while in other areas small settlements were springing up around old trading posts and Mounted Police forts.

In Edmonton, the first newspaper in the area was published, a small tabloid printed on a hand press carried overland from Winnipeg. Closer to Crowfoot's domain, Fort Macleod and Fort Calgary still were tiny communities of traders, policemen, and mixed-bloods. But signs of imminent change were everywhere. The federal government, in an attempt to put the prairies to use, had announced a new grazing policy which would allow ranchers and speculators to lease up to one hundred thousand acres of former Blackfoot hunting grounds for a cent an acre a year. Already, eastern Canadian and British syndicates were surveying land and looking to the Montana and Wyoming ranges for cattle and crews. At the same time, track already was being laid near Winnipeg for the new transcontinental Canadian Pacific Railway. No one knew whether it would go through the prairies or farther north past Fort Edmonton, but either way it was bound to affect the isolated Blackfoot tribes.

As the winter of 1881–82 approached, Crowfoot's biggest worry was the ration situation, which continued to deteriorate. Contractors and government employees became more arrogant; there was not enough food, and practically no game re-

139

mained to supplement the meager rations. A few buffalo were sighted, mostly in herds of two or three, but they were wild and hard to find. In all the years after the Blackfeet returned to the Crossing, they killed only fifty of the animals, while the Bloods managed to find just thirty-five, the Piegans forty, and the Sarcees fifteen.[1] This was a mere handful when compared to the millions which had once roamed the area.

Crowfoot tried to tell the government men on his reserve that the situation was desperate and that his people were hungry, but his pleas fell on deaf ears. Twice during October and November he went to the farm instructor, the senior government man, and demanded more rations. Each time he was turned down and, as if to undermine his position, the instructor reported to the Indian agent that Crowfoot had headed a "demonstration" to "intimidate" him.[2]

Agent N. T. Macleod, who lived a hundred miles away at Fort Macleod, visited the Blackfoot Reserve early in November to pay the annual treaty money; there he criticized Crowfoot for his actions, warning him not to cause any further trouble.

However, the situation continued to worsen. Twice in November the contractors, I. G. Baker and Company of Montana, ran out of beef and flour. Each time they had to cut down or in some cases stop giving out rations until more food could be brought in. The haphazard system made the starving Blackfeet uneasy, and rumors circulated that this was the first step in cutting off their rations entirely. Crowfoot, lacking the advice of his friends among the Mounted Police, was as suspicious as the rest and felt that the white men on his reserve could not be trusted.

[1] Indian Agent N. T. Macleod to John A. Macdonald, superintendent general of Indian affairs, Fort Macleod, December 31, 1881, in the Blood Correspondence, Vol. 2, 110.
[2] Macleod to Dewdney, December 10, 1881, *loc. cit.*, Vol. 2, 101.

In December, the resentment and uneasiness took on a more dangerous tone when some Blackfoot warriors threatened to shoot the government men if rations were not increased. As in the late buffalo days, the Black Soldiers took a leading part in the demonstration. Crowfoot, in an attempt to resolve the situation, led another delegation to see the farm instructor. The chief said that, when the rationing had been handled by the Mounted Police, a fair share had been given to all. But now that it was in the hands of civilians, the number of ration tickets had been drastically cut. Some railway surveyors who were working in the district offered to check the lists for Crowfoot, but the farm instructor would not let them enter the building.[3] He also refused to increase the rations but instead offered the chief some gunpowder to use in hunting for his own food.

Crowfoot's failure did nothing to ease the anger of the Blackfeet, and the discontent finally resulted in some of the warriors firing several shots at the log ration house while the instructor was giving out meat and flour. The instructor immediately fled from Blackfoot Crossing and carried news of the trouble to the Indian agent in Fort Macleod. The officer commanding the fort was notified and a detachment of ten Mounted Policemen under Inspector Francis J. Dickens was dispatched to protect the government employees.[4] When they arrived, the men took over a small Indian Department warehouse as their headquarters.

Their presence had a quieting effect, although in the eyes of Crowfoot the police lost much of their prestige. He felt that the Blackfoot complaints had been justified and that the police should have made an investigation. He remembered Colonel Macleod's promises of equal treatment for all the queen's subjects and wondered if, after all, the police might have one law for the Indians and another for the whites.

[3] *Ibid.*, December 12, 1881, Vol. 2, 113.
[4] *Ibid.*, p. 104.

The climax to the troubles came on the day after New Year, 1882. The tension and resentment which had been building up for months culminated in an incident which almost became a tragedy. The abusive attitude of the government employees had not changed during the presence of the Mounted Police; neither did their practice of selling heads and offal.

On this particular day, a minor chief named Bull Elk had given a dollar to W. T. Barton, an employee, as payment for a steer's head. Barton, however, refused to sell it, as he thought there was too much meat on it, and gave the money back. The chief, angered by the curt treatment, picked another head and gave his dollar back to one of the employees. Then, while waiting for his wife to help him carry it, he found that the head had been sold to someone else and was gone. He managed to have the head returned, but as he started to carry it away he was ordered off the premises by employee Charles Daly. Bull Elk argued that he had paid for the head, but Daly accused him of stealing. In the scuffle that followed, Daly snatched the head from Bull Elk's wife and later took it away from the chief himself.

Angrily Bull Elk stalked back to his lodge and grabbed his rifle. Returning to the ration house, he saw Daly hanging out some fresh hides and, although the chief still was over a hundred yards away, he fired two shots toward the government building. The first bullet struck the logs several feet from Daly while the second one went wild.

The Mounted Police were notified and Inspector Dickens went with two men to arrest Bull Elk. They found him, but a howl of protest arose from the Blackfeet when the police began to take him to their detachment. The resentment against the government employees had reached a fever pitch, and the action of the police in arresting Bull Elk had been too much. As Dickens and his men escorted the prisoner across the flats, the crowd grew and the inspector saw that the Black Soldiers had placed guards on all the trails.

Fearfully, Dickens sent a hurried message to Crowfoot and tried to force his way through the angry crowd. However, the Indians pulled Bull Elk free and, in the scuffle that followed, Dickens was knocked to the ground. This heralded a fresh outburst, and shots were fired into the air. When Crowfoot arrived a few minutes later, he angrily proclaimed that Bull Elk was innocent and should never have been arrested. He was as angry as the rest of his people and would give no help to the police. He told them that some of the white men had treated the Indians like dogs.[5] Seeing that it would be impossible to hold Bull Elk, Dickens agreed to leave him in Crowfoot's custody until a magistrate came to try the case. This satisfied Crowfoot, and he told the crowd to go home before there was any more trouble.

As soon as he had a chance, the badly frightened Dickens sent an urgent message to Fort Macleod explaining the dangerous situation. Superintendent Crozier immediately set out with a party of twenty men and upon his arrival at Blackfoot Crossing found the excitement still running high. Crozier's first action was to have Bull Elk rearrested and to give him a preliminary examination.

When Crowfoot heard that the police had broken their agreement, he was angered and shocked. He had expected dishonesty and duplicity from the low class of white civilians on the reserve, but not from the queen's soldiers. Stalking out of his camp, he saw that the Black Soldiers had stirred the warriors into a state of near hysteria and that most of them were armed with rifles, knives, or bows and arrows. When he got to the police detachment, Crowfoot was even more disturbed

[5] Inspector Dickens to Superintendent Crozier, January 3, 1882, in *Sessional Papers of Canada*, 1882, No. 18, 50.

at the actions of the Red Coats. Sacks of flour had been piled outside the warehouse to form breastworks, and loopholes had been cut in the walls so that the police could shoot from inside. The whole building had been turned into an improvised fort.

Crowfoot boldly marched to the police barricade and demanded that Bull Elk be returned to his custody as was originally agreed. Crozier refused and told the chief that the prisoner would be taken to Fort Macleod for trial. Angry and distrustful, Crowfoot asked if they planned to fight. "Certainly not," was the reply, "unless you commence."[6]

The next day the armed patrol took Bull Elk to Fort Macleod, where Colonel Macleod was the magistrate who heard the case. As Crowfoot had claimed from the beginning, there was no real case against Bull Elk. The Indian agent, when reporting the affair to his commissioner, commented that "the evidence was conflicting. No intent of doing bodily harm could be shown. Harsh treatment and hard words were shown to have been used towards the Indians, giving them cause of complaint."[7]

However, Bull Elk had been guilty of using his weapon in a threatening manner and was given the lightest possible sentence, fourteen days in the guardhouse. "It has been a nasty business," Colonel Macleod confided to his wife.[8]

The implications of the case were far greater than were first apparent. This was the first time that Crowfoot had encouraged active defiance of the Mounted Police. He had seen the incident in its proper perspective, but because of the one-sided treatment given to the white employees by the police the case had gotten out of hand. Crowfoot lost much of his respect

[6] John Peter Turner, *The North-West Mounted Police, 1873–1893*, I, 631.
[7] Macleod to Dewdney, January 12, 1882, in the Blood Correspondence, Vol. 2, 114. Details of the case also are given in *Sessional Papers of Canada*, 1882, No. 18, 50–55, and in Denny, *The Law Marches West*, 172–73.
[8] Turner, *op. cit.*, 631.

for the Mounted Police because of the incident, and this was to have a bearing on his future relations with the government. In breaking their word with Crowfoot and in refusing to take any action upon the legitimate complaints of his people, the Mounted Police lost one of their most influential supporters. The aura of infallible justice which Crowfoot had attached to the Mounted Police, and which had meen maintained by such men as Colonel Macleod, had been destroyed in a single thoughtless act.

If any man realized the seriousness of the situation, it was Indian Commissioner Dewdney. Acting decisively, he replaced the farm instructor with a former policeman, William Pocklington, a man who was liked by the Indians. He also relieved Indian Agent Macleod of his responsibilities among the tribe, and for a replacement he appointed Crowfoot's old and trusted friend, Inspector Denny. But these changes had come too late. Never again would Crowfoot place his blind trust in the Mounted Police or, for that matter, in any white man.

After a brief investigation on the Blackfoot Reserve, Agent Denny agreed with Crowfoot that the situation was most unsatisfactory. He took immediate steps to put the rationing in the hands of reliable men and stopped the practice of selling beef heads and offal. He found also that the Indians had been expected to plant their own gardens and crops in the spring, but they had not been provided with the proper tools or seed. In short, he found the situation to be even worse than Crowfoot had originally claimed.

Denny's efforts in the next few weeks brought the first settled conditions on the reserve since the Indians had returned from Montana. He persuaded Old Sun and his followers to move farther upstream, where he built a separate ration house for them. He issued the Indians axes and encouraged them to build log houses to replace their worn tipis. He made sure the contractors brought in enough flour to last for a year as visible proof that the government did not intend to let the Indians starve and generally did everything possible to regain the trust of the tribe.

However, the situation did not last. In the late spring, several inexperienced eastern Canadian men were given political appointments on reserves in the area, and the old problems arose anew. The man placed on the Blackfoot Reserve was, according to Agent Denny, "a young man . . . who had never seen an Indian before that month, not capable of taking charge of them. . . ."[9] His inefficient handling of the situation only added to the distrust of Crowfoot and the other chiefs. Most of the employees whom the Indians liked resigned, and before midsummer the situation had again become serious.

Frustrated, Crowfoot led a delegation of eight chiefs to Fort Macleod to see Agent Denny. He asked why the new men were there and why the ones he trusted were gone. Denny tried to explain, but the complex dealings and political favoritism of the Indian Department could not be told in a way which could satisfy the chief. All that Denny could promise was that as long as he was in charge he would be their friend and would try to help them. And, true to his word, he was able to have the officious easterner transferred and to turn the agency back to Pocklington. While it did not entirely solve the problems, it brought a relatively settled condition to the reserve for the rest of the summer.

As he had promised Lord Lorne, Crowfoot did his best to become a farmer. He planted a small field of turnips and potatoes during the year, but it was only a token effort to set an example for the younger men. In this he was successful, for

[9] Denny to Dewdney, Fort Macleod, July 28, 1882, in the Blood Correspondence, Vol. 2, 133.

by the end of the year the Blackfeet had produced fifty tons of potatoes as well as quantities of turnips and barley.[10]

Events had moved rapidly since the Blackfeet had settled on their reserve. Confused by their new life and angered by their treatment at the hands of the government, the Indians saw each new change with distrust. Even the erection of mission buildings by the Roman Catholics and the Anglicans was looked upon with some doubt.[11]

It was not surprising, therefore, when the news was circulated that an iron road would be built past their reserve that the Blackfeet were suspicious. They were told of a great fiery machine that would carry white people into the country, but this fire wagon was beyond their comprehension. Crowfoot asked Agent Denny about it and got his assurance that it would help the Indian people. Denny explained how it would bring food to the Blackfeet and enable the officials to visit them more often.

In the spring of 1883, surveyors for the Canadian Pacific Railway swarmed into the area and began to lay out the lines for the tracks. Stakes were driven and mounds erected across the open prairies from Medicine Hat and past the northern fringe of the Blackfoot Reserve. The roadbed also went through the old reserve which originally had been set aside for the Bloods and Sarcees. Feeling that he still had a claim to the

[10] Annual report of C. E. Denny, November 10, 1882, in *Sessional Papers of Canada*, 1883, No. 5, 173.

[11] When an Anglican missionary tried to establish a mission in Crowfoot's camp near the new Roman Catholic church, the request was denied. "Crowfoot . . . said that since one Church had been built all the old men & women & children had died & if another Church was built, all would die. They had too much church." (Rev. J. W. Tims to Rev. C. C. Fenn, September 6, 1883, in Canadian Missionary Society Papers, microfilm in Glenbow-Alberta Institute Archives, Calgary.) As a result of this interview, the Anglicans went to Old Sun's camp to build their church.

area, Crowfoot again went to Agent Denny and voiced his complaints. He had been told by the Crees that the survey mounds marked the places where white men's houses would be built and that the line was being put through his old reserve without his permission. Denny took the chief out to the right-of-way and tried to explain the reason for the mounds and the stakes, but Crowfoot, now distrustful of the government, was not convinced that the project would be to his tribe's advantage.[12]

A further complication arose in May when the first grading crews arrived and pitched their camp beside Crowfoot Creek, just outside the reserve. Many of the men were coarse and rough and, although the Indians were warned to stay away, prostitution soon became a problem.

As the rumors of discontent spread, Father Lacombe was sent to the reserve, where he distributed two hundred pounds of tea, as well as sugar, flour, and tobacco provided by the Canadian Pacific Railway in an attempt to quiet the agitated tribe.[13] A few days later Edgar Dewdney, who now was lieutenant governor of the North West Territory as well as Indian commissioner, visited them and called a council meeting with Crowfoot. As a result of these meetings, the chief reluctantly agreed to surrender any claims he might have to the abandoned reserve and to let the rail line pass along the northern fringe of the tribal lands. It was a decision he later was to regret, for the speeding locomotives, belching smoke and sparks over his reserve, caused nothing but trouble.

Also, some of the Indians were angry with Crowfoot for having made the agreement; some even claimed that he had been bribed by the railway. One rumor was spread that he

---

[12] Annual report of C. E. Denny, July 20, 1883, in *Sessional Papers of Canada*, 1884, No. 4, 84.

[13] Hughes, *Father Lacombe, the Black-Robe Voyageur*, 274.

had been given seven hundred dollars a year for letting the railway go through and that the money was divided among his personal followers.[14] Another story was that all the chiefs agreed to the location of the line, but Crowfoot was given a gift of seventy dollars a month for his permission to build the stations of Gleichen and Cluny adjoining the reserve.[15]

The stories were not true, but they indicated how bitterly some of the people felt about the railroad. As suspicious as he was, however, Crowfoot initially believed Denny's claim that the line could bring food and help to the tribe in times of need. In later years, Crowfoot became an outspoken critic of the railway and refused to co-operate further with its representatives. He would not let them build a fence along the reserve right-of-way or a spur line to the Blackfoot coal mine. Neither would he let them dig a trench to install an underground pipeline from the Bow River to Crowfoot Siding.

He also demanded compensation for the tribe several times when trains caused prairie fires and claimed he had been misinformed by the railway about its value to his people. ". . . the Canadian Pacific Railway said that the road running through the reserve would not do any damage to them," the Indian agent reported Crowfoot as saying, "but it had," and the tribe would have to be compensated before he would give any concessions.[16] In 1887, when one of Crowfoot's own horses was killed on the right-of-way, he demanded seventy-five dollars compensation, but he could not collect it. A year later he still was trying and even had reduced his evaluation to fifty dollars.[17]

Crowfoot's new life on the reserve was having a bad effect

[14] Interview with Many Guns by Hanks, about 1939.
[15] Interview with Duck Chief by Hanks, about 1939.
[16] Agent Begg to Dewdney, April 18, 1888, in the Selected Papers, 152. Correspondence relating to his other complaints are in the same volume.
[17] *Ibid.*, November 19, 1887, 142.

on him. Not only was he becoming cynical, but the meager diet and the continual bickering was affecting his health. Crowfoot never had been a strong man physically and was frequently bedridden during his early years on the reserve. He became sick during an erysipelas epidemic in 1883 and for a time it appeared that he would not live. He blamed the sickness on the smoke from the trains and his warriors, hearing the news, told Crowfoot that if he would give the word they would tear up the tracks and drive the railroad people away.[18] The Mounted Police heard about the threat and sent a detachment of men to the chief's lodge on the pretense of looking after him until he recovered. This stopped any further agitation, and at one stage, when Crowfoot felt he might die, he advised his people to follow the peaceful path he had set for them. Although he distrusted many of the whites, he said the Blackfeet were forced to depend upon the government for food.[19] Fortunately, the chief recovered, although his general health continued to decline during the next few years.

Crowfoot's position in the camp had changed drastically since the nomadic days. Now that his people depended upon the government for food, they knew that his was the only voice which could bring them help. In the old days, a minor chief always could get food for his followers, but now Crowfoot was the only provider. His fellow head chief, Old Sun, was old and feeble, and it was Crowfoot whom the officials always came to see. His oratory, his dignified manner, and his tremendous influence captured the imagination of almost every white man who met him. At the same time, although often under pressure from officials, he had not become a "government Indian." In fact, after he lost faith in the Mounted Police,

[18] Article by Archdeacon John W. Tims in the *Calgary Daily Herald*, April 29, 1933.

[19] *Calgary Herald*, May 7, 1885.

the number of white men who had any influence over him was reduced to a mere handful. Most prominent among these were Colonel Macleod, Cecil Denny, Governor Dewdney, and perhaps Father Lacombe. He knew he could trust them, but no one knows the actual amount of influence they wielded over him. Another white man who was close to the chief was Jean L'Heureux, the French-Canadian renegade who had lived in Crowfoot's camp since the buffalo days. His position, however, appeared to be that of an interpreter rather than adviser.

But Crowfoot's over-all faith in the white man was shaken by the events on his reserve, and more and more he became susceptible to the stories of Indians and mixed-bloods who visited his lodge. In his role as peacemaker, he had made many friends among the Crees, Assiniboines, and mixed-bloods, as well as among his own nation. Much to the consternation of the government, he welcomed to his camp such turbulent old friends as Big Bear, Little Pine, Bob Tail, and other intractable leaders who were unhappy with the way their people were being treated farther north.

During these early years of the 1880's, Crowfoot was not the wealthy man he had been in the buffalo days, but he still had more horses than most of his fellow chiefs and, because he received gifts or additional rations from visiting officials, he often had extra food for the needy. The young men who had worked for him in the old days usually camped nearby and performed any necessary chores. They herded his horses, carried messages, and, in a limited way, tried to maintain their old life.

These years also were busy ones for Crowfoot, for there were frequent disagreements and disputes which had to be settled. A few years earlier, such problems often were resolved by the dissidents traveling their own separate ways until their tempers cooled. But now, thrown together in a semipermanent existence for the first time in their lives, the Blackfeet had to adjust to the new conditions. No longer could a young warrior steal another man's wife and flee to another camp, nor could a man suspected of using evil medicine leave the band for a few months. Instead, they were tied to the ration house and the reserve, so Crowfoot had to take the role of mediator and magistrate. He listened patiently to the problems of his people, gave them counsel, and succeeded in maintaining relative harmony in the camps.

It was not an easy task, but one which required the chief's constant attention and energy. And in spite of the bigger problems of rations, railways, and the very future of the Blackfeet, he always found time for individual disputes and problems.

Crowfoot continued to live in his tipi and spurned suggestions that he build a log house. His wives, children, and old blind mother lived with him; his favorite wife, Cutting Woman, usually traveled with him on journeys to other reserves. His foster brother, Three Bulls, had formed his own band but still was under the influence of the head chief, for in maturity he lacked the ability required of a good leader.

In dress, Crowfoot combined the old and the new. Castoff pieces of clothing were given to him and, except when he donned his scarlet treaty uniform, he usually wore a white man's shirt and trousers, a Hudson's Bay blanket, moccasins, and the faithful owl's head in his hair. He was not a vain man like many of his people and often left his long hair hanging free over his shoulders rather than braiding it into two neat strands.

From his position, Crowfoot watched the developments in the West with interest. He listened to the disturbing words of his Cree and mixed-blood visitors and learned how the mixed-blood farmers were afraid that the government would take away their lands. He heard that the northern Crees were being given inferior bacon instead of rations of beef and that they blamed this food for the sickness in their camps.

With his faith in the white man faltering, Crowfoot heard these stories and pondered over them. His adopted son, Pound-maker, would receive the same treatment as the other Crees, and, while some of the stories were fanciful ones, others came from the lips of Indians he knew and trusted. These were the tales that worried him the most.

CHAPTER FOURTEEN

DISCONTENT

The small gardens and fields dotting the river bottom, the rough log shacks mingled with canvas or worn leather lodges, the deeply rutted trails that went from camp to camp—all these were visible evidence of the harsh new life of the Blackfeet. Skin robes were worn over ragged cloth shirts, Hudson's Bay blankets covered tattered buckskin coats and leggings, and the seeds of frustration and discontent were sown deeply in Blackfoot hearts. The sudden and complete loss of the buffalo, the utter poverty unlike anything they had ever seen, and the continual double dealings of the queen's representatives had made many of them feel that the white man was following a program to wipe them off the face of the earth.

During this time, the Black Soldiers had gained a solid following and, although they had again come under the influence of their head chief, they were ready to believe anything bad about the white man. Each time an incident occurred which upset their daily routine, the warriors immediately were suspicious and gathered in their camps to discuss the news.

Late in 1883, Big Bear sent a messenger to the Blackfoot camps suggesting that a grand council be held on their reserve next summer. The Cree chief wanted to form an alliance and to talk over plans for stopping the trains from passing through their lands. The messenger was welcomed into Crowfoot's lodge and the head chief listened with sympathy to his list of complaints against the whites. The Blackfeet generally favored such a council with their onetime enemies, but Crowfoot withheld his decision until the messenger had visited the

Bloods and Piegans. The plans did not materialize, however, for the Mounted Police intercepted the courier at the Blood Reserve, ordered him back to his own reserve, and informed the chiefs that no such council would be permitted.[1]

But sympathies for the Cree cause had been aroused, and in the months that followed Crowfoot had visits from several other messengers. They were not part of any pre-arranged plot but often were old friends from the buffalo days who wanted an audience. Crowfoot, with his great reputation and influence, was the natural one to be approached, and he in turn listened to the visitors' words and watched as the Indian Department officials and Mounted Police tried to keep these men away. He did not petition the government on their behalf, but he withdrew more and more from his white associates and never turned a Cree or mixed-blood visitor away from his lodge.

By 1884, the government, Mounted Police, and settlers were firmly in control of the Canadian prairies. Yet the unrest continued. Many of those leading the dissent were mixed-bloods who had found the Red River area intolerable after the 1869–70 rebellion. Others were local mixed-bloods and white settlers who had made repeated representations to Ottawa about their land rights but had received no reply.

One of the main problems was recognition of lands which had been settled before surveys were made. The mixed-bloods in particular were concerned, because their land was laid out in the French river-lot system, with long narrow farms fronting on rivers and lakes. The Canadian government, on the other hand, was slicing up the country into neat sections, each one mile square, and there was no assurance that the mixed-blood farms would not be swallowed up in the surveys.

The center of the unrest was along the North Saskatchewan

[1] Denny to Dewdney, December 25, 1883, in the Blood Correspondence, Vol. 2, 149.

River near Prince Albert and Battleford. While this was more than two hundred miles from the Blackfoot Reserve, the intervening prairies were vacant, traveled only by the occasional hunting party, which brought the latest news of the unrest to Crowfoot's camp.

In the spring of 1884, the mixed-bloods were so alarmed by the land situation that they sent a delegation to Montana to seek out Louis Riel, their exiled leader. Now an American citizen and schoolteacher, he agreed to return and to resume the fight for his people's rights. As Riel left his little school in Judith Basin for the last time, messengers were dispatched to spread the news. One of these men, a French-Cree mixed-blood named Bear's Head,[2] was sent to Blackfoot country, particularly to see Crowfoot. On his journey north, Bear's Head met a hunting party of Blackfeet near the settlement of High River and told them of his mission. His conversation was overheard by a Mounted Police scout, and the mixed-blood was arrested before he reached Blackfoot Crossing.

In court, when Bear's Head admitted he was from the Judith Basin in Montana and had just left Riel's following, the magistrate sentenced him to jail for a month on a charge of vagrancy. News of the courier and his imprisonment soon reached Crowfoot. Vagrancy was a charge which had no meaning to him; he could understand a man being jailed for theft or murder, but to sentence a person who had done nothing was beyond his understanding. This caused a vague uneasiness among Crowfoot and his suspicious warriors.

After the month had passed, Bear's Head was set free and ordered to leave the district, but instead he went directly to Crowfoot's lodge. There he was given a warm welcome and stayed as a guest of the chief. In councils with the chiefs,

[2] In a report in the *Calgary Herald*, June 18, 1884, this man was referred to as Bear's Hand.

Bear's Head used his imprisonment to stir the fires of unrest among them. He told them that the country was still theirs, as the government had not kept its promises, and there was no reason for the Blackfeet to go hungry; the cattle which roamed the plains were rightfully theirs, since the white men had destroyed the buffalo.[3] He told them that the white men should be driven out and the whole country kept for the exclusive use of the Indians and mixed-bloods. In many ways, it was a repetition of Riel's self-government aspirations which Crowfoot had heard and rejected four years earlier.

But times had changed in those few years. Crowfoot had seen promises broken; even the treaty seemed to have a different meaning from the way he had understood it in 1877. He had signed because of his faith in the Mounted Police, but now this was gone. He still believed the queen was his friend but noted that Riel's plan did not call for his people to leave her protective wing. Rather, they would remain as her subjects but without the yoke of the white man's government cast upon them. Where Crowfoot previously had scoffed at Riel's words, he now listened to those of his messenger. Where he once had offered to send an army against anyone who tried to oppose the police, he now listened to the words of revolt.

To add to the unrest in the Blackfoot camp, the bands had congregated into a single camp for the annual Sun Dance. Here the glorious days of the past were relived as warriors told of their raids against the enemy, the killings, the scalpings, and the horses taken from unwary camps. They remembered the happy days when they lived off the buffalo and depended upon nothing else for their daily food. Those were the days which had ceased only a few years before but now seemed like a dream.

During the few days which the mixed-blood messenger spent

[3] Steele, *Forty Years in Canada*, 180.

in their camps, Blackfoot attitudes underwent a noticeable change. Previously they had been disgruntled, but still they worked their tiny gardens and grumbled among themselves. But the combination of rebellious talk and the Sun Dance changed their attitudes so much that the Indian agent went to Calgary for help. He told the Mounted Police that the mixed-blood was on his reserve and said that "the former friendly demeanour of the tribe had changed to one of sulkiness and hostility."[4]

Surprised that Bear's Head still was in the district, Inspector S. B. Steele sent a sergeant to arrest him for disturbing the peace. Arriving at Gleichen, the policeman saw that the Sun Dance was in progress and wisely decided not to interfere. Instead, he persuaded a friendly Indian to lure the mixed-blood to the station, where he clapped him in irons and took him on the next train to Calgary. During the trip, the prisoner was unshackled and in an unguarded moment he made a successful dash for freedom. The escorting policeman tried to follow, but in jumping from the train he dislocated his knee.[5]

Colonel Irvine dispatched Inspector Steele and two constables in pursuit on the following day. The trio followed the trail for about sixty miles and a day later rode to Old Sun's camp, where they learned that the fugitive had gone back to the Sun Dance.

It was raining hard when the police party approached the Sun Dance camp, so they stopped in front of Crowfoot's lodge without being seen. When Steele went into the tipi he found a group of chiefs sitting around the fire. To the left of Crowfoot, in the position of honor, was the mixed-blood courier. Speaking through an interpreter, Steele said that he had come for the man and was taking him to Calgary to face trial. Then,

[4] *Ibid.*, 181.
[5] *Calgary Herald*, June 18, 1884.

knowing that Bear's Head understood English, he repeated the statement directly to the escaped prisoner.

Crowfoot replied in an angry torrent of Blackfoot, which the frightened interpreter said were words of defiance and hostility. By the nods of approval, it was obvious that Crowfoot had the support of his council. Steele replied harshly to the chief and made certain his message was interpreted exactly as he said it, without temporizing with the chief. Crowfoot sprang to his feet and rushed toward the policeman, but Steele, with his hand on the butt of his revolver, waved him back. He then grabbed the mixed-blood by the collar of his shirt and hauled him outside. He was no sooner placed in the police buckboard than the white men were surrounded by several hundred hostile Indians. Already inflamed by the stories which had been circulated, the Indians were waiting only for a signal from Crowfoot to rescue the mixed-blood courier.

Inspector Steele ordered the interpreter to tell the warriors that when the Mounted Police came to arrest a man, whether Indian or white, nothing would stop them.

> I told Crowfoot to come out of the tent so that I could speak to him, and that I had to have the half-breed dead or alive . . . that he, Crowfoot, had behaved badly, although he had always received fair play, that he acted as if he had been treated unjustly, whereas he had received the greatest kindness from the Mounted Police and all of the officers of the Indian Department, and was making a poor return for it. . . .[6]

The inspector told the crowd that the mixed-blood was a liar and that he wanted Crowfoot to go to Calgary to see the man put on trial. "You will find that you have been harboring a disturber of the peace," he told them.

Assured that he would be able to attend the trial, Crowfoot let the police take the prisoner away; four days later he had

[6] Steele, op. cit., 184.

the grim satisfaction of seeing Bear's Head acquitted of all charges against him. However, on a request from the magistrate, the mixed-blood agreed to leave the district immediately. The only results of the whole incident had been to convince the Indians that Riel's messenger had been an honest man whom the Mounted Police had badgered until he was forced to leave the country. The incident also had forced Crowfoot to choose sides, and he had no hesitation in supporting the mixed-blood agitator rather than the police. He did so not because one was Indian and the other white but rather because one was right and the other wrong. Crowfoot judged men by their honesty, and in this incident the magistrate had fully vindicated the chief's choice. And if the mixed-blood's actions were honest, how was Crowfoot to judge his words?

Governor Dewdney was disturbed when the incident was reported to him; in an effort to appease and impress the disgruntled chiefs, he invited them to visit the cities of Regina and Winnipeg. This was the first long trip that any of them had made on the railroad and, except for war raids in their younger years, it was the first time they had been outside of Blackfoot country.

The chiefs chosen to go were Crowfoot and Three Bulls of the Blackfeet, Red Crow of the Bloods, and Eagle Tail of the Piegans. The main reason for the tour was to offset "the influences brought to bear upon the Indians of Treaty 7 with a view of prevailing upon them to join in a general stand against the government."[7]

While in Winnipeg, they went on a tour of the city and later visited some of their people imprisoned in the Stony Mountain Penitentiary. Within a few days they saw hundreds of white

[7] Dewdney to Indian Department, July 19, 1884, in the Macdonald Papers, North-West Rebellion, Vol. 1, 95. Also No. 14624 in the Indian Affairs Archives.

men who lived within a few days' travel of Blackfoot country and they saw street after street of brick buildings and houses, which were visible proof of the white man's strength.

Planning this tour was perhaps the wisest move of Governor Dewdney's career, for until this time most of the Blackfoot chiefs had gauged the strength of the whites by the tiny villages in their own areas. They believed that most of the white men in the world already were in their country and these could easily be wiped out by their warriors. If a few more did come, there would not be enough to cause any trouble. But in Winnipeg and Regina Crowfoot and the other chiefs saw the true strength of the invader. Winnipeg alone had a population of more than fifteen thousand, with enough men and weapons to defeat the entire Blackfoot nation.

Crowfoot essentially was a man of peace, but frustration and anger had caused him to listen to and consider the words of rebellion from the other tribes. He had sympathized with the Crees and mixed-bloods and was disillusioned by the way his own followers had been treated. But now, with clear evidence of the white man's fighting strength before him, he realized that open defiance would result only in the destruction of his tribe. While he may not have wanted the domination of the white man, he saw there was no escape from it other than annihilation. At the same time, he recognized that there were many good white people and that through them he could try to correct the injustices and build a new life for his people.

Crowfoot returned to the reserve a wiser man, determined to co-operate with the government agents. But, as in the past, the western officials no sooner solved one problem than administrators in the federal capital stirred things up again. This time they tampered with the delicate subject of rations, which, while still not plentiful, were sufficient to prevent starvation. In looking over the ration lists, the economy-minded officials saw that the northern Crees took most of their meat in the form of bacon, which was cheaper than fresh beef, while the plains tribes in Treaty Seven received most of their meat ration in beef. Officials felt that such extravagance was unnecessary, so a directive was sent out that for two days out of every seven, the Blackfeet were to receive bacon instead of beef.

The Indians acted with the same degree of violence on all reserves. At the Blood Reserve, an angry chief hurled the bacon into the face of the issuer while the Black Soldiers refused to let anyone take their rations. Red Crow demanded that beef be issued and accused the government of breaking the promises made at the treaty. On the Piegan Reserve, Eagle Tail would not accept the meat and, having once been shown a live pig, refused to believe bacon came from that animal. Crowfoot, having the same distaste for the smoked meat as his fellow chiefs, refused to accept it and sent a protest to Governor Dewdney. "He says they will die if they eat bacon in summer," reported the agent, "and in my opinion they don't want much of it in winter."[8] As a result of these protests, the government postponed further bacon issues, but made no effort to improve the general low scale of rations. Indian Agent Denny was so disgusted by these shortsighted economy moves that he resigned from the government. "The cutting down of rations on Indian reserves both north and south, all at once, had a disastrous effect," he commented.[9]

As the winter of 1884–85 approached, the seeds of unrest from the Saskatchewan country again were scattered among the Blackfeet. While Crowfoot was in Calgary to see a white doctor, his old Cree friend Little Pine came to the reserve, ostensibly to trade horses but really to gain sympathy for the

[8] Begg to Dewdney, August 6, 1884, in the Selected Papers, 11.

[9] Cecil E. Denny, *The Riders of the Plains; a Reminiscence of the Early and Exciting Days in the North-West*, 182.

Cree and mixed-blood cause. He complained that his people were starving and that the Blackfeet were being treated just as badly. He also brought a message from Big Bear, who said that the tribes should unite in a common cause and eventually live together in a large community on the Red Deer River.[10] Little Pine said that when spring came the Blackfeet should leave their reserve and travel north for a grand alliance.[11] Some of the Blackfoot warriors announced that they would join and told the Cree chief that Crowfoot was not satisfied with the way he was being treated.[12]

Little Pine was pleased with the reception and promised that upon returning north he would send messengers to the other Cree camps to tell them the news. He then would send a courier to the Blackfeet with more information about the alliance.[13] On his return to the north, Little Pine reported his success to a large gathering at Duck Lake; as evidence of friendship, he had five horses given him by the Blackfeet.

During the winter, Crowfoot was ill again and was forced to stay in bed for over a month, anxiously watching the events which were gaining momentum around him. The only news which really helped him during his recuperation was a message from Poundmaker. It said that Big Bear had been camped with him for most of the summer and that the agitation was spreading among the Crees and mixed-bloods. Poundmaker wanted to get away from the disturbances in the Battleford area and, as soon as the grass was green, he would come for a long visit to the Blackfoot Reserve. The grass would be green in April, 1885.

[10] Begg to Dewdney, August 6, 1885, in the Selected Papers, 22.
[11] Denny, *The Riders of the Plains*, 192.
[12] J. W. Rae to Dewdney, January 24, 1885, an enclosure in letter from Dewdney to Macdonald, February 14, 1885, in the Macdonald Papers, North-West Rebellion, Vol. 107.
[13] S. P. Bellendine to Dewdney, January 2, 1885, No. 17936 in the Indian Affairs Archives.

CHAPTER FIFTEEN

REBELLION

The role of Crowfoot in the Riel Rebellion of 1885 was one of the most complex of his life. He was neither as completely loyal to the government as claimed by Indian Department officials nor as secretly treacherous as feared by white settlers. Much of the conflict took place in Crowfoot's own mind and, torn as he was between several firm allegiances, he emerged from the episode not so much as a leader who would not raise his hand against the white population but more as a wise but ailing chief who was concerned only about the welfare of his tribe.

Riel had spent the winter of 1884–85 near Prince Albert and Batoche, urging the Canadian government to act on a petition of the mixed-bloods. They wanted their land claims confirmed, provinces formed, lands sold to build schools and hospitals, and their people given direct aid. The petition, in the form of a Bill of Rights, was sent to Ottawa, where it was ignored. In the meantime, tension built up in the West until, in March, 1885, Riel finally decided to form his own provisional government. From there, it was only a short step to open insurrection, which occurred when Riel's men seized trading stores and took prisoners in the settlement of Batoche. This action was followed by a skirmish with the Mounted Police, and the rebellion was under way! Within days, volunteers were being recruited in eastern Canada, while western communities prepared for war.

When news of the outbreak reached Crowfoot, he found himself in an unenviable position. On one hand, he was a peaceful man who had seen the large settlements of Manitoba and knew in his heart that the rebels were fighting a losing battle. On the other hand, his sympathies were firmly with the insurgents, many of his warriors were anxious for battle, and his adopted son was in the center of the conflict.

The first news of the rebellion came to the Blackfeet as fantastic tales of great victories by the mixed-bloods over the police. Hundreds of white men had been slaughtered with few native losses; stores had been pillaged and burned, food supplies captured, and Riel had established his new government. Scouts and runners constantly were in touch with rebel sources, and it was not uncommon for the Blackfeet to learn of a battle hours or days before the information was telegraphed to government officials.[1] The news often was distorted, but, for that matter, so were the stories given them by the white men. Each side tried to impress the Blackfeet with their victories.

At the first news of the outbreak, the Blackfoot Indians became very excited. A few who had lost friends or relatives to Cree raiders in the buffalo days still had no sympathy for their old enemies, but others were anxious to join the fight against the whites. The younger warriors were particularly eager and might have started for the north had they not been stopped by Crowfoot.

One of the leaders in favor of joining the fight was Big Plume, the influential chief of the Liars band. With a solid following of young men behind him, he went to Crowfoot's lodge and presented him with a small bundle consisting of

[1] Anglican missionary J. W. Tims commented, "By some means the Blackfeet were kept well informed of what was going on & often had news by their own couriers as soon as we by telegraph." (Tims to Rev. C.C. Fenn, October 23, 1885, in the Canadian Missionary Society Papers.) F. C. Cornish, an agency clerk, recalled how the Blackfeet received news of Riel's surrender a full day before the message came over the wires. ("Blackfeet and the Rebellion," *Alberta Historical Review*, Spring, 1958.)

tobacco, sweetgrass, and bullets.[2] If Crowfoot had built an altar of prairie sod, burned the sweetgrass on it, and smoked the gift of tobacco, it would have indicated his willingness to fight. The chief, however, would not accept the offer and finally persuaded the warriors to stay at home. He wanted to find out what was really happening in the north and to learn if the Bloods and Piegans intended to join before taking any direct action. Hopefully, a number of Indians went to Calgary to buy cartridges, but the shopkeepers refused to sell them.[3]

Father Lacombe, who was in charge of an Indian industrial school at nearby High River, publicly proclaimed the loyalty of the Blackfoot Indians, but privately he had his doubts. As he recalled later:

> . . . the Blackfeet were well armed with rifles and they had plenty of cartridges. Among the Indians of the North-West there was a kind of general feeling, with the old and the young, that the time was at hand to finish with the white policy. Many influential Indians were at the time fomenting the fire of rebellion.[4]

Crowfoot welcomed all Cree messengers into his camp, but he would not smoke the tobacco which was offered to him. Instead, he sent messengers with tobacco to the Bloods and the Piegans, asking if they intended to join in the battle. Running Wolf, a Piegan war chief, was in favor of rebelling and ordered the young men to quit working in their fields in preparation for their next move.[5] However, head chief Eagle Tail was firmly against joining the fight and gradually won the dissidents over to his side.

[2] Interview with One Gun, March 5, 1957.
[3] *Calgary Herald*, March 26, 1885.
[4] Lacombe, "A Great Chieftain," *Macleod Gazette*, May 22 and 29, 1890.
[5] Agent Pocklington to Dewdney, May 31, 1885, in the Blood Correspondence, Vol. 2, 194.

Among the Bloods, Red Crow refused to accept Crowfoot's tobacco.[6] His people still were enemies of the Crees and, unlike Crowfoot, the Blood chief had retained his trust in the Mounted Police and the government. Red Crow sent the tobacco back to the Blackfeet while Bull Shield, a minor chief, announced to the agent, "Give us ammunition and we'll show you how soon we can set the Crees afoot and lick them."[7] At this time, the Bloods could raise many more warriors than the Blackfeet and were only a few miles from the American border, where ammunition could easily be bought. Crowfoot respected Red Crow's opinion and, more often than was realized, he relied upon it in making decisions which affected the whole nation.

However, the situation at Blackfoot Crossing did not change with the news of the Blood's hostility. The chiefs knew that if the Crees and other tribes succeeded, many young Bloods would desert their leaders for the glory of battle. Rumors also circulated that several tribes in Montana were expected to cross the border to join the rebellion.

In southern Alberta, the citizens of Calgary heard rumors of a Blackfoot attack on their town. In desperation a messenger was sent to High River to get Father Lacombe, as they felt he was the only man in the district who might be able to pacify the tribe. A Canadian Pacific engine was made available to the priest and took him, accompanied by interpreter Billy Gladstone, to Gleichen station. There he was met by the acting Indian agent. By the time he had toured Old Sun's and

[6] "It was reported to me by an Indian that some little time since 'Crowfoot' had sent tobacco to 'Red Crow' to join him and make a common cause with the Crees against the whites, but that 'Red Crow' sent the tobacco back. . . . I believe it to be true, notwithstanding Crowfoot's assurance of loyalty. I am much more inclined to believe 'Red Crow' than 'Crowfoot.'" (Pocklington to Dewdney, May 10, 1885, in the Blood Correspondence, Vol. 2, 188.)

[7] *Ibid.*, April 6, 1885, 184.

Crowfoot's camps, he was certain that the rumors were false. In his council with the chiefs, the priest warned them not to believe all the reports they had heard about the troubles in the north, but to stay peacefully on their reserve. He then returned to Gleichen and sent a reassuring telegram to the prime minister. "I have seen Crowfoot and all the Blackfeet. All quiet. Promised me to be loyal no matter how the things may turn elsewhere."[8]

The Blackfeet had learned about the false scare through their alert scouts and, while the hurried trip by the priest may have relieved the fears of the Calgary people, it only added to the already dangerous situation which existed on the reserve. "The people in Calgary are in a state of panic," complained the acting agent, "and are doing the very thing calculated to raise a disturbance, viz: letting the Indians see that they are apprehensive of danger. I saw the Mayor and told him to tell the people to be less excitable."[9]

However, the incident reminded Governor Dewdney that the Blackfeet, if aroused, could add to the already explosive uprising. He therefore appointed their good friend, Cecil Denny, as his personal representative in Treaty Seven, with full powers over the existing agents. Knowing the plight of the Indians, Denny immediately increased the rations of beef and flour. He realized that they were less likely to rebel if their stomachs were full and that to go to war would mean a loss of rations, which, prior to the increase, were not sufficient to matter. The generous chunks of beef and bags of flour would do much to keep peace in the tribe. To leave no room for com-

---

[8] Telegram, Lacombe to Macdonald, March 30, 1885, in the Outgoing Telegrams from the North-West, 1885, 23, at the Glenbow-Alberta Institute Archives, Calgary.

[9] Report for March, 1885, W. Sherwood, acting agent, to Dewdney, in the Selected Papers, 25.

plaint, Denny also increased the rations to the Bloods and Piegans.

As the events of the rebellion unfolded, Crowfoot knew he had been right to keep his people at peace. The Bloods would not rise, the Blackfeet were happier now that the rations had been increased, and there still was a strong core of old warriors who wanted no part of a Cree fight. They claimed that the northern tribes, the mixed-bloods in particular, could not be trusted.

The Crees continued to come to Crowfoot's camp, some as refugees but others as messengers or agitators. They told how easy it was to kill a soldier or policeman in battle. Whenever their leaders were shot, they said, the white men would flee and would shoot over their shoulders without taking aim. In that way they often killed their own men. When they sat down to eat, they would leave their guns standing on end in the middle of the camp, and the Indians could wipe them out before they could even get to them.[10]

The presence of Cree couriers and refugees in the Blackfoot camps helped to keep the unrest alive. New arrivals brought more stories of northern victories. The battle at Fish Creek, the victories of Big Bear at Frog Lake and Fort Pitt, and other skirmishes were known to the Blackfeet almost as soon as they happened. Each time they learned of a white man's defeat, they cheered the rebel forces. A trader told the police:

> The whole of these tribes had runners carrying tobacco from tribe to tribe, all united as one man watching [Fort] Macleod on all sides, and ready at any moment to pounce upon it and massacre every white man, woman and child. . . . Had Riel won a victory over our troops [at Batoche], the whole of these tribes would have poured in to sweep the N.W. Ter-

[10] Interview with Ayoungman, January, 1958.

ritories—Macleod first—relying on the ranches to supply necessary food. . . . No old chief, even Crowfoot, would have been able to restrain their people . . .[11]

As the rebellion entered its second month, none of Crowfoot's followers had been drawn into the fray. The Crees and mixed-bloods had expected them at the very beginning, but, when neither the Blackfeet nor the American tribes appeared, some of the rebels became angry with them.

On April 11, a council was scheduled between the Blackfoot chiefs and Governor Dewdney. Crowfoot still was sympathetic to the rebel cause but had made no public statement about his feelings. A day or two before the council, a Cree messenger came to Crowfoot's camp to seek help. He told Crowfoot that either he must join the rebels or his people would be wiped out by the Crees. If he refused to join, the Crees would win their northern battles and then march to Blackfoot Crossing to cut off the railway and destroy his tribe.[12] Nothing could have aroused the chief's fury more than that kind of crude threat, and he angrily ordered the messenger out of his camp. When news of the possible invasion leaked out to the nearby settlements, Crowfoot stalked over to Gleichen station and informed the section men he would provide a hundred warriors for their defense if any Cree army came near them. He also offered the French-Canadian storekeeper the protection of his own lodge if there was any danger of an attack.

Crowfoot was therefore in a receptive mood when Governor Dewdney, Agent Denny, Father Lacombe, and interpreter Gladstone arrived. They were met at Cluny station by Crowfoot and 150 mounted Indians and escorted the five miles to

[11] Interview with Hugh Munro by A. Jukes, 1886. Jukes Papers, Glenbow-Alberta Institute, Calgary.
[12] Telegram, *Calgary Herald* to *Winnipeg Free Press*, April 10, 1885, in the Outgoing Telegrams from the North-West, 1885, 97.

the Roman Catholic mission where the council was to be held. Governor Dewdney explained the purpose of this trip and, having heard about the Cree threats, promised that the government would always protect its faithful subjects. He said the Blackfeet must shut their ears to all rumors they might hear about the Crees coming to attack them. The soldiers, now entering the country, were not going to hurt the Blackfeet but punish the bad Indians for killing the whites. There was nothing to fear as long as they remained faithful to their treaty.[13]

Crowfoot heard the words with satisfaction. It was the first time since the outbreak of the rebellion that anyone in authority had promised protection and help for his people. He solemnly shook hands with each of the officials, eloquently pledged his loyalty to the queen, and promised that his people would not cause the government any harm. He said, with the true artfulness of a native politician, that if the government wanted to help the Blackfeet, his tribe was ready to do all it could. He also promised to do his utmost to see that the Bloods remained at peace. The speech revealed Crowfoot's remarkable talent in dealing with the white man. He knew the government was worried about his tribe but realized it would be a poor time to air petty complaints or make extravagant demands. He kept his speech on a high plane of loyalty and co-operation, using words which would win the support of his white friends.

Later in the day, the chief dictated a message which was telegraphed to John A. Macdonald, the prime minister.

On behalf of myself and my people I wish to send through you to the Great Mother the words I have given to the Governor at a Council held at which all my minor chiefs and young men were present. We are agreed and determined to remain loyal

13 *Calgary Herald*, April 16, 1885.

171

to the Queen. Our young men will go to work on their reserve and will raise all the crops we can and we hope the Government will help us to sell what we can raise. Continued reports and many lies are brought to us and we don't know what to believe, but now that we have seen the Governor and heard him speak, we will shut our ears and only listen to and believe what is told to us through the Governor. Should any Indians come to our reserve and ask us to join them in war, we will send them away. I have sent messengers to the Bloods and Piegans who belong to our treaty to tell them what we are doing and what we intend to do about the trouble. I want Mr. Dewdney to be with us and all my men are of the same mind. Words sent by Father Lacombe I answered: We will be loyal to the Queen whatever happens. I have copy of this and when the trouble is over will have it with pride to show to the Queen's men and we leave our future in your hands. We have asked for nothing but the governor has given us a lot of presents of tea and tobacco. He will tell you what other talk we had at our Council. It was all good, not a bad word.[14]

The message was received with satisfaction by the prime minister. The names of Crowfoot and the Blackfoot tribe were known to the eastern public and, with his North West policies under attack, Macdonald was happy to release some good news. The message was read to the cabinet, where it received hearty applause, and was passed on to Lord Lansdowne, the governor general, for transmission to the queen.

Three days later, the prime minister's reply was flashed across the wires to Gleichen and interpreted to the chief.

I have received your good and loyal message by telegraph and I have shown it to the Governor General who is our Great

---

[14] Crowfoot to Macdonald, April 11, 1885, in the Outgoing Telegrams from the North-West, 1885, 107–108. There are a number of variations between this manuscript telegram and the one eventually released to the public. Another version is given in George F. G. Stanley, *The Birth of Western Canada*, 361–62.

Unloading beef at the Blackfoot ration house. From a contemporary engraving.

174

Indians at Fort Calgary. The man sitting in the chair is Inspector
Cecil Denny, who strove constantly to ease their lot.

Poundmaker, Crowfoot's adopted son, was the official guide to the Marquis of Lorne, governor general of Canada, on his visit to the West.

When meeting dignitaries, the Blackfeet men were mounted. The women and children stood respectfully in the distance.

The Canadian Pacific Railway during construction.

Gleichen Station.

Crowfoot and other leaders of the Moccasin band in council. This
sketch was made by an artist accompanying the Marquis of Lorne.

Crowfoot and his family in 1884. All the children in the picture had died of tuberculosis within two years.

Louis Riel, who swept the Crees into his rebellion in 1885 but failed to win the support of Crowfoot.

Poundmaker with visiting French journalists during his imprisonment at Stony Mountain Penitentiary.

Blackfoot chiefs in Ottawa. Crowfoot, in the center, with Three Bulls, his foster brother, on the left, and Red Crow, the Blood chief, on the right. Father Lacombe and Jean L'Heureux stand behind them.

Crowfoot in Ottawa.

Red Crow, whose allegiance to the whites helped Crowfoot remain loyal.

Crowfoot. The twist of hair on top of his head held an owl's head.

Three Bulls, Crowfoot's successor as head chief of the Moccasin band of the Blackfoot tribe.

Chief under the Queen. He desires me to thank you for your promise to be a faithful friend of our Great Mother and is sure your words are true. I have also read your message to our great Council at Ottawa which pleased them very much. What Governor Dewdney has promised shall be performed. We will help you to sell what you cannot use of your crop and shall never forget the good conduct of yourself, your minor chiefs and warriors.[15]

The visit of Governor Dewdney and the message from the prime minister convinced Crowfoot that the future success of his tribe lay with the white men, not the insurgents. His heart still yearned to help his adopted son, but he could not sacrifice his own people for a personal cause. He heard with sadness of the unprovoked attack on Poundmaker's camp by Colonel Otter and how his chieftain son had turned the tide of battle. Armed only with a whip, he had been an inspiration to all those around him and had forced the white attackers to withdraw. Then, showing the results of Crowfoot's teachings, he had refused to let his young warriors pursue and destroy the retreating soldiers. This fight at Cutknife Hill had been a victory for the Indians, but in the weeks that followed hundreds of militiamen poured into the Saskatchewan country from Manitoba and eastern Canada, turning the early tides of battle. With their arrival, the defeat of the Crees and mixed-bloods was only a matter of time.

Crowfoot realized that the Cree messenger who had threat-

[15] Macdonald to Crowfoot, April 14, 1885, in the Outgoing Telegrams from the North-West, 1885, 133. Upon receipt of this wire, Agent Begg made a quick summary of its contents and reluctantly sent it to Cecil Denny, the special agent whom he felt was interfering with his own duties. "The good words of Crowfoot are appreciated by the big chiefs at Ottawa. The loyalty of the B'feet will never be forgotten. Crowfoot's words shall be sent to the Queen. All Mr. Dewdney's promises shall be faithfully carried out." (Selected Papers, 28.) This condensation later was published as being the actual message received by Crowfoot.

ened him had been a tactless orator. The rebel cause was a just one and, while he was not interested now in joining it, he still gave it his full sympathy. Cree refugees were welcome in his camp, even when officials tried to drive them away. He had pledged his loyalty to the queen and would keep his promise, but it would not stop him from feeling sorry for those whom he thought were being badly treated.

There still was a remote chance that some of the Crees might want to attack his camps, and he knew his people did not have enough ammunition to put up a good fight. Remembering Governor Dewdney's promise of help, he went to the Indian agent and asked for a small amount of ammunition. A coded wire was sent to Dewdney, recommending the request, but it was turned down.[16] Crowfoot was disturbed when he learned of the refusal, and again the rumors began to circulate. Some thought the Blackfeet were to be left defenseless so the Crees could attack them; others felt the soldiers would come to their camps as they had to Poundmaker's and try to slaughter them.

Later in April, when the first troops of eastern soldiers came to Calgary, the Blackfoot scouts reported their every move. The posting of a company of Winnipeg Rifles to Gleichen, Cluny, and Crowfoot stations heightened their anxiety, and a short time later this turned to alarm when a party of militiamen under Major Hatton swept through the Blackfoot camps at night while on a patrol.[17] This resulted in a general distrust of the strangely uniformed men.

Crowfoot's attitude during the rebellion worried Father Lacombe and, while the priest publicly assured everyone that the chief would remain at peace, he did not fully trust him or

[16] Begg to Dewdney, April 16, 1885, in the Selected Papers, 29.
[17] Denny, *The Riders of the Plains*, 205.

his tribe. Several weeks after the council he sent a confidential report to Governor Dewdney voicing his suspicions.

For my own part, what I have seen of the Blackfeet and their kindred since last Spring makes me believe that if they have been quiet and have made loyal promises during the Cree rebellion, it was purely out of self-interest in order to get more and more out of the Department.

From the beginning of the war, one who knows the Indian character could very easily perceive they were not pleased when told of the victories of the whites; on the contrary they were sorry and disappointed. Crowfoot received into his camp and fed for months many Cree families, and was very much displeased when we tried to send away these Crees . . . Crowfoot and his people have been and are still yet very indignant because they were refused ammunition.

. . . I tried every means in my power to keep these savages from doing any mischief to the whites and to prevent any rising. The Indians in this part seem not at all afraid of the soldiers. All that display of troops along the C.P.R. line . . . has not yet convinced them that the government is powerful. The fact is they seem and act as if they despise the red and blue coat, perhaps more than before. . . .[18]

Lacombe's assessment was an extremely accurate one, but he, like others of the period, expected Crowfoot to be faithful to the whites. They could not understand that his only allegiance was to the Blackfeet and, if he co-operated with the Mounted Police or Indian Department officials, he did so only because it would help his people. If he had ever believed that the welfare of the Blackfeet would be improved by attacking the white man, he would not have hesitated. But unless there was a drastic change in the course of the rebellion, Crowfoot's personal loyalty to the government was assured. The knowl-

[18] Macdonald Papers, Vol. 212.

edge that the Crees would be defeated, together with the increased rations and the promises of the prime minister, all made it sheer folly for the Blackfeet to rise.

During May, 1885, as the rebellion moved into its period of most bitter fighting, Crowfoot's interest shifted to the problems in his own family. One of his daughters began coughing blood and was placed under the care of a medicine man. The chief offered two horses as payment to the Indian doctors, and for several days the lodge reverberated with the boom, boom, boom of the drums and chanting of the holy men. For more than a week they remained at the little girl's side, but her coughing grew worse and, on May 29, she died.[19]

This was his second child to die in three years, a boy having passed away in 1883. In mourning, Crowfoot gave away most of his clothes and blankets, and in sadness he traveled sixty miles west to the Sarcee Reserve, where he stayed for some time. By then, there was no doubt in his mind that the rebellion was lost and the Crees defeated. Among them, somewhere in the ravaged bushlands, was his adopted son, Poundmaker. Crowfoot, his own health deteriorating during the period of mourning, quietly watched the final events of the rebellion, as Big Bear was defeated, Riel was captured, his followers dispersed, and refugees fled to Montana. His only action during those final days was to send messages to the Bloods and Piegans asking them to show mercy toward refugee Crees who were passing through their lands.

When the rebellion ended in June, Crowfoot was sick, unhappy, and loyal to the government. His people had remained at peace, and throughout Canadian circles Crowfoot was being proclaimed a hero. Locally, those who knew the chief were not so sure. As it was expressed in one newspaper:

[19] Begg to Dewdney, May 30, 1885, *loc. cit.*

192

When Crowfoot talked to the Governor-General about his loyalty, he evidently forgot several incidents connected with the late rebellion. . . . it is pretty well known that he was in full sympathy with Poundmaker. Yes, Crowfoot kept loyal, but this is just about all he did do. He did that by good luck more than by good management. . . .[20]

If events had been different, Crowfoot might have joined the rebellion. If the railway had not passed so close to his reserve and given him such proof of the white man's strength; if Red Crow and his Blood warriors had agreed to go to war; if he himself had not made a tour of Winnipeg and Regina; and if Agent Denny had not acted with such speed and decisiveness. There were many ifs, each having its effect upon the chief. Crowfoot would have liked to lead his people into a war to drive any evil and corrupt white men from his land. Instead, he let his rifle remain idle and his knife stay in its scabbard. At all times he was unswervingly loyal, not to the government, but to his own people. This was his only reason for remaining at peace.

[20] *Fort Macleod Gazette,* October 13, 1885.

CHAPTER SIXTEEN

DEATH OF A SON

By June, 1885, the rebels were beaten, the dreams of native self-government were shattered, and the white man had become unchallenged master of the Canadian West. Poundmaker was in jail, refugees were fleeing into Montana, and everywhere was the chaotic aftermath of a brief but bitter war.

When Crowfoot learned that his adopted son would face trial in Regina, he sent an anxious letter to Governor Dewdney asking for mercy.

> I, Crowfoot, having lately heard that Poundmaker has been arrested and taken to Regina for having been connected with the rebellion, I wish to say that I sent word to him to remain loyal, but my words did not reach him until he had been persuaded into joining the half-breeds. He being my adopted son and we having been together a great deal in past years, I have great affection for him and would request the Great Mother, through her Chiefs in Regina, as a personal favor to me, to grant him pardon, with the understanding that he remains loyal in future and I promise to use my influence to the same end.[1]

Now that the rebellion was over, Canadians were screaming for the blood of those who had led the fight, so Crowfoot's request was turned down. The Cree chief stood trial, even though evidence indicated that he had done his best to avoid conflict and to save the lives of any whites who became prisoners of the insurgents. He had taken his followers to Battleford

---

[1] Crowfoot to Dewdney, July 27, 1885, interpreted by Jean L'Heureux and witnessed by Agent Begg, in the Selected Papers, 51.

when they were hungry and tried to get their regular rations, but the Indian agent had fled, and the chief was powerless to stop the pillaging which followed. Later, in Colonel Otter's unprovoked attack at Cutknife Hill, only through Poundmaker's actions did the white force avoid annihilation. He had been loyal to his people but, unlike Crowfoot, he had wanted to protect the whites even during the height of the rebellion. He told the court:

> I am not guilty. A lot has been said against me that is untrue. I am glad of what I have done in the Queen's country. What I did was for the Great Mother. When my people and the whites met in battle, I saved the Queen's men. I took the firearms from my following and gave them up at Battleford. Everything I could do was to prevent bloodshed. Had I wanted war, I would not be here but on the prairie. You did not catch me. I gave myself up. You have me because I wanted peace. I cannot help myself, but I am still a man. You may do as you like with me.[2]

Poundmaker, the adopted son of Crowfoot, was found guilty and sentenced to three years in Stony Mountain Penitentiary.

When the Blackfoot chief received the news, he was too sick to be angry. He had been bedridden for several days and was feeling the effects of the old musket ball his body still carried as a souvenir of his warring past. His condition was so grave that the Indian agent feared for his life and said that "if he died, it would be hard to replace him."[3]

During the rest of the summer, Crowfoot carried out some of his duties, but his illness, the imprisonment of Poundmaker, and further sickness in his family made him surly and short-tempered. He helped the Mounted Police obtain the surrender of some horse thieves, one of whom was his son-in-law, but his

[2] Turner, *The North-West Mounted Police, 1873–1893*, II, 244.
[3] Begg to Dewdney, August 29, 1885, in the Selected Papers, 59.

health was too poor for any active participation in daily life. In October, when the treaty payments were made, Crowfoot was presented with one hundred dollars from a thankful government "for keeping loyal."[4]

Early in December another of Crowfoot's children died of tuberculosis, leaving him with only three children in his own lodge. This was pathetically different from the twelve children who were crowded into his tipi at the signing of Treaty Seven. Some had since grown up and left him, but most of them had died. Crowfoot again was confined to bed, but on Christmas day, when he learned that another of his children was ill, he went to the Indian agent to be assured that Poundmaker was still alive and well. The agent took down a message from the sick chief and forwarded it to the penitentiary.

> Dear Poundmaker, I send you word that the Agent and other white men say you are well used, and I should like you to send word if it really is true. . . . I have such a feeling of lonesomeness of seeing my children dying every year and if I hear that you are dead, I will have no more use for life. I shake hands with the Agent and Mr. Dewdney, and I know they will do what they can for you. I would like to hear from you direct, how you are treated. Your father, Crowfoot.[5]

The reply, which was received early in January, did much to hearten the ailing chief. Poundmaker assured his father that he was being well treated and had no complaints. With it was a message from Governor Dewdney, giving his sympathy to Crowfoot for the tragedies in his family and promising to visit Poundmaker to see that he was well.

The winter of 1885–86 was a mild one on the Blackfoot Reserve, but it also was a hard one. The Canadian Pacific trains, belching sparks as they thundered past, set one prairie fire after

[4] Voucher, Blackfoot Crossing, October 1, 1885, *loc. cit.*, 65.
[5] Crowfoot to Poundmaker, December 25, 1885, *loc. cit.*, 75.

another until the whole area was a blackened ruin. Crowfoot tried to get compensation for the tribe, but the Montreal company took no action. The impatience of the chief started more rumors of war. These were pounced upon not only by sensational newspapers but also by those who were eager to heap further discredit upon the prime minister's Conservative regime. Politically, the western rebellion had been a severe blow to his party, and the execution of Riel as a traitor had opened a wide rift between English and French Canada.

Rumors were spread that the Bloods were joining with American tribes to make common war on the whites. An alliance between the Kutenais, Stonies, and Blackfeet was proclaimed. As the stories spread, they became wilder and more fanciful and all predicted a rebellion in the spring of 1886. The *Toronto Mail* sent its top reporter, George H. Ham, to Blackfoot Crossing to check the facts. He arrived about a week after Crowfoot had received Poundmaker's letter, so the chief was in good spirits. The reporter quoted him as saying:

> Why should the Blackfeet create trouble? Are they not quiet and peaceable and industrious? The Government is doing well for them and treating them kindly, and they are doing well. Why should you kill us, or we kill you? Let our white friends have compassion. I have two hearts—one is like stone, and one is tender. Suppose the soldiers come and, without provocation, try to kill us. I am not a child—I know we shall get redress from the law. If they did kill us, my tender heart would feel for my people.[6]

The rebellion and the tragedy in his family had wrought many changes in the great chief. He was fully resigned now to the domination of the white man, but at the same time he knew that some were really sincere about trying to help his

[6] Maclean, *Canadian Savage Folk*, 376.

people. He was willing to work with these officials to aid his tribe in accepting the life which had been thrust upon them. He still balked at some of their proposals but no longer had the heart nor desire to fight. Some of the spark went out of the chief during the rebellion year, and from that time on he withdrew more and more into his personal life. Only on special occasions would he rise above his sickness, sadness, and sense of defeat to give dynamic leadership to his tribe. He had led the Blackfeet through the plains, into a treaty, and onto a reserve. Now he found that the controls were in the hands of those who issued rations and gave out treaty money. Like every other chief in the country, he could choose between being a leader without power and a chief who would break loose from his chains and in the process destroy his people. His choice, governed largely by his illness, was to give the Blackfeet all the diplomatic leadership he could provide. But, realistically, he no longer tried to run the reserve. This was being done by Indian Agent Magnus Begg, whom Crowfoot found to be an honest and dedicated man.

In February, Governor Dewdney took the first step to gain Poundmaker's release from prison. He dispatched a telegram to Begg, asking him to get a letter from Crowfoot. On the strength of this plea, Poundmaker was set free on March 4, after serving only about six months of the three-year sentence. He no longer was a handsome and dignified leader but a man whose health had broken down completely in those few months. One of the reasons for the quick release was the fear that he might die in jail. When he went back to his own reserve, Poundmaker was met with hatred by the surrounding white population. For five weeks he rested, then set out for Blackfoot Crossing to see his beloved father. There were three in the party—Poundmaker, his wife, and a young nephew. It took them nine days to cross the open prairies to the Blackfoot

Reserve, as they had only one horse among them; the others had been seized after the rebellion. On May 21, the man who had been convicted of making war against the queen stopped wearily in front of Crowfoot's lodge.

The chief was happy to see Poundmaker, for less than a month earlier the son who had been sick since Christmas had died of tuberculosis, while another was confined to bed and was not expected to live.[7] Saddened by these further tragedies in his family, Crowfoot welcomed the son whom he had never expected to see again.

Early in May, the other sick child passed away, leaving only one baby daughter at home, two daughters who were married, a grown son who was going blind . . . and Poundmaker. The Cree chief was the only son who had reached manhood without being disabled or deformed, so it was upon him that Crowfoot bestowed all his fatherly love and affection. For the first time in weeks the chief was happy and alert. He recovered from the illnesses which had plagued him since the rebellion and was pleased when the time came for the Sun Dance. When a messenger came from the Gros Ventres in Montana asking if he would join them in a fight against the American soldiers, he laughed it off.[8] He sent the young warrior back with the advice that the Gros Ventres should forget about fighting and settle down to their new life.

Poundmaker's health also improved during the weeks in Crowfoot's lodge, so it was with sadness that the Cree chief finally announced that he must return to his own reserve to build a new life for his followers. He would stay only until the Sun Dance was under way.

Situated on the flats near the Bow River, the great Sun Dance camp was an impressive sight. Hundreds of lodges were

[7] *Lethbridge* (Alberta) *News,* April 2, 1886.
[8] Begg to Dewdney, June 31, 1886, in the Selected Papers, 101.

pitched in a great circle, with the brush-covered holy lodge in the center. Crowfoot, as always, was camped with the Moccasin band and, although he did not join in the sacred rites, he favored this type of religion over anything the white man had to offer.

On July 4, Crowfoot and Poundmaker were guests at one of the ceremonies where holy food of thick saskatoon berry soup and bannock was passed to each man. As Poundmaker sipped a spoonful of soup, something became lodged in his throat and he started to cough violently. Suddenly the blood gushed from his mouth and in a few moments he was dead.

The doctor's diagnosis was that a burst blood vessel had caused the death. The Blackfeet, however, had their own theories, based upon their religious beliefs. According to one tale, when Poundmaker was released from prison some of his people said he should have been hanged. Worried about their threats, he went to a shaman, who said he would have a good life as long as he did not eat any saskatoon berries. When he was handed the bowl at the Sun Dance, he said, "I think I'll take a chance," but when he took one swallow he died.[9]

Crowfoot was grief-stricken by the loss. His only healthy son was taken from him during a year when all his children were dying. In a few months his lodge had become an empty shell where there was only sadness and mourning. His favorite son, his most beloved son, was dead.

[9] Interview with Joe Crowfoot, March 4, 1957.

CHAPTER SEVENTEEN

TRIUMPHANT TOUR

Two weeks after Poundmaker's remains were placed on a hill overlooking the Bow River, the prime minister and his wife came to see Crowfoot. It was a respectful meeting between two great chieftains, Sir John A. Macdonald on his way to the Pacific on the newly completed railroad, and Crowfoot in rags of mourning. The old chief appreciated the visit of the prime minister and said he would like to visit the white leader in his Ottawa home.

The opportunity came sooner than he expected. An impressive monument had been erected to honor the Mohawk leader Joseph Brant in Brantford, Ontario, and the government decided to bring a number of western chiefs to the unveiling. This would serve the combined purposes of showing the people of eastern Canada the great chiefs who had remained loyal, and, in case they harbored any doubts, it would show the western Indians that Canada was a powerful nation. The chiefs picked for the trip were Crowfoot and Three Bulls, Red Crow of the Bloods and his young relative One Spot, North Axe, son of the deceased Piegan chief Eagle Tail, and four Cree chiefs, Osoup, Starblanket, Big Child, and Flying in a Circle.

Father Lacombe, still doubting Crowfoot's role in the rebellion, opposed his going east on the tour. After a visit from the priest in January, the prime minister wrote that "he is very much opposed to Crowfoot's coming East, for what reason I don't know."[1] However, when the final decision was made in favor of the trip, Lacombe asked for permission to bring Crow-

---

[1] Macdonald to Dewdney, February 28, 1886, in the Macdonald Papers.

foot and Three Bulls ahead of time so they could attend a
bazaar in Montreal's St. Peter's Cathedral. When Governor
Dewdney approved, the Blackfoot chief started his triumphant
tour of the eastern provinces. With his foster brother Three
Bulls and interpreter Jean L'Heureux in tow, he was the center
of attention for the two weeks that he remained in the East.

Crowfoot was weak and tired from his illnesses but welcomed the chance to leave his reserve and visit the great land
to the east. It was customary for men in mourning to get away
from their unhappy homes, so the invitation had come at an
opportune time. A year earlier, the chief had refused to take
a trip to Winnipeg because his children were ill. Now it did
not matter, for they were dead.

The party left Blackfoot Crossing on September 25 and upon
their arrival in Montreal were taken to the Richelieu Hotel,
where a crowd of reporters waited for them. Crowfoot was
somewhat bewildered by the mob and turned to the priest for
advice. Knowing only his native tongue, he could not understand the words of the eager men who hurled questions at
him. When queries about the rebellion were interpreted, he
commented that many inducements had been offered him to
join the insurgents, but he and his tribe had remained loyal.

During their four days in Montreal, Crowfoot and Three
Bulls attended the bazaar and were shown the many sights of
the fine city. They were escorted to the docks, taken aboard
a boat to shoot the Lachine Rapids, and from there went to a
convent and to the Bank of Montreal. At the Canadian Pacific
Railway headquarters, they met Sir George Stephen, William
Van Horne, T. G. Shaughnessy, and all the others who had
taken such an active part in building the railway. Mr. Van
Horne welcomed the chief and, as a gift for remaining loyal
during the rebellion, presented him with a perpetual pass on

the line. No mention was made of the misery and problems the railway had caused the Blackfoot tribe.

The strain of the activities was beginning to have its effect on the chief, and more and more he relied on the guidance of Father Lacombe. The next day, when the priest said he must leave them and go to Ottawa, Crowfoot was alarmed at the idea of being stranded in the huge city and asked him to stay. Only after Father Lacombe promised to return that night did the chief let him go. That day, the two chiefs were taken on a short tour of the city but returned to their rooms at noon to await the return of the priest. Although interpreter L'Heureux was still at his side, Crowfoot apparently placed little faith in him.

On Sunday, October 3, the visitors left for Quebec City, where they stayed for three days. They went to the provincial parliament buildings, where they were introduced to the lieutenant governor and other high officials. The governor made an impressive speech to the great chief and presented him with a silver medal bearing the inscription *Donnée a Sapomaxico, Pied de Corbeau, 1886* on one side and the governor's coat of arms on the other. The tour then continued through the government library to the legislative chamber, where Crowfoot was invited to sit in the speaker's chair. The chiefs were introduced to the premier and, before leaving for lunch, they went to the Livernois photography studio. After lunch the party went to the Quebec Citadel, where Crowfoot was greatly impressed with the cannons, the strong defenses, and the guards in attendance. This part of the tour was arranged to give the visitors some idea of the white man's strength.

The Indians were impressed by the many strange sights in the white man's world and often asked interpreter L'Heureux to buy interesting objects for them. During the tour they asked for a small steamboat, a baby carriage, a lady's saddle, a piano, an electric light, a monkey, zoological and museum specimens, and "a machine to make thunder."[2]

Four days later Crowfoot arrived in Ottawa, where he met fellow chiefs Red Crow, One Spot, and North Axe, who had just arrived. The chieftain also was heartened with the news that Father Lacombe would take them all to see the prime minister during the afternoon.

On their way to Sir John's residence at Earnscliff, the party struggled through the Saturday crowds at Byward market place, where the rural folk brought their produce for sale. Crowfoot watched with interest and amusement as vegetables, chickens, and other goods were bartered by the industrious farmers. Arriving at Earnscliff, Crowfoot greeted Sir John as "Brother-in-Law" and Lady Macdonald as "Good-Hearted Woman," the names he had given them during their western tour.

In one of the few speeches made during the trip, Crowfoot said:

> We have come a long way to see you at your house, and our own are far far off. We remember you both when you came to us in our land this summer. We had a good feeling there, and the lady gave our people money and presents. We hope the Great Chief will think of our people. Since the white man came the buffalo have gone away, and now we need to be helped by the white chiefs. We want big farms, but what shall we do with what we cannot eat? I see this morning that you do not forget your own people, as they sell what they do not want. That is what my people want to do.[3]

[2] L'Heureux to Dewdney, July 22, 1887, No. 32864 in the Indian Affairs Archives.

[3] *Montreal Daily Herald*, October 11, 1886.

Sir John presented each of the chiefs with twenty-five dollars and promised to send presents and clothing to their people when they returned to their reserves. He urged them to remain at peace and not grow impatient if all their needs were not granted at once. In conclusion, he promised that Governor Dewdney would look after them and help them to market their surplus grain and vegetables.

Before the chiefs left, Crowfoot told the prime minister that the tour of Montreal and Quebec had made him ill and begged to be permitted to go home, as he was not well enough to continue the journey to Brantford. Reluctantly Sir John agreed.

The next day was Sunday, and, with Father Lacombe as their guide, the chiefs were taken to High Mass at the basilica. The priest himself conducted the service, which was in French, as well as addressing a few words in the Blackfoot language. He spoke of the good work of Crowfoot among the Indians of the West and of his tremendous influence for good. During the remainder of the afternoon the chiefs toured the cemeteries, where Crowfoot admired the great respect which the white people had for their dead.

On Monday, a levee was held at the City Hall by Crowfoot and the other chiefs, and, after an address by Mayor F. McDougal, a gift of fifty-one dollars was presented to the chief. The money was divided, and Crowfoot spoke on behalf of his comrades at his last official function in eastern Canada. Completely fatigued, he returned to his hotel to await the train home.

Early in the week, Red Crow, North Axe, One Spot, and the newly arrived Crees left for Brantford, while Crowfoot, Three Bulls, and Father Lacombe boarded the train for the West. They stopped briefly at Winnipeg to see Archbishop Taché and again at Regina to see Governor Dewdney. When they finally left the territorial capital, a reporter at the station noted that the chief was not so meticulous about his dress and did not appear to be well.

> Crowfoot was negligently but elegantly attired in an ultra-marine eight-point blanket and a hard hat neatly decorated with a golden rose and band, whilst Three Bulls stuck to the striped blanket and the beaver cap of his forefathers. Both chiefs wore store clothes of the most fashionable cut, and judging their hurry to take the trail, were glad to be once more on their way home. Their trip has been a very arduous one for them, their simple stomachs being unaccustomed to the luxurious feed of the effete east, and it will take them several weeks to recover from the dyspeptic attack caused by a too liberal indulgence in civilized diet in the halls of the great. . . .[4]

On October 20, a tired Crowfoot returned to his reserve. His happiness to be back knew no bounds as he embraced his relatives and officials of the Indian Department who were at the station. A large supply of beef, tea, tobacco, sugar, and rice from the prime minister was distributed to the Indians, and Crowfoot began to relate his experiences. It would take a month to tell all that he had seen, he said to his friends.

During the trip, Crowfoot came to realize that his previous attitude toward the white people had been right and that, while the government had many employees who worked against his people, the majority of whites wanted only their friendship. The inefficiency, callousness, and contempt which he had faced during his few years on the reserve were not part of a plan to destroy his people; they were merely the expressions of individuals. Had Crowfoot been a healthy man, a new era of progress and co-operation might have been born. But he was tired, sick, and, although only fifty-six, already an old man.

[4] *Ibid.*, October 19, 1886, in an article from the Regina correspondent.

CHAPTER EIGHTEEN

END OF AN ERA

While Crowfoot had been in the East, more tragedy had struck his family; one of his foster brothers had died. Crowfoot again went into mourning and in his grief his health declined. A hacking cough shook his thin body, bringing blood to his mouth, and he became a near recluse with no desire to work or to leave his home. His only action during the winter of 1886–87 was to prepare a petition on behalf of his old friend Edgar Dewdney, who was in danger of losing his appointment as lieutenant governor. While signed by the whole council, it had been sponsored by the head chief, who had always valued his friend's honesty and faith.

In February, 1887, feeling that a change of scenery might do him some good, Crowfoot went south onto the prairies that he had not seen for several years. A hundred and fifty miles away he was welcomed to the Blood Reserve and to the lodge of Red Crow. The chief found that the Bloods had become much different from his own people. They still had the air of wild freedom about them and constantly traveled back and forth across the line to visit their South Piegan neighbors in Montana. At the time of his arrival, the young Bloods were waiting for the snows to melt so they could make war on the Gros Ventres in Montana. Red Crow was opposed to the raid, but he was almost powerless in the face of his young warriors' frenzied excitement. Crowfoot immediately joined him in the role of peacemaker, and together they tried to calm the excited tribe. They succeeded in gaining the support of some old people, but most of the younger ones were in favor of war.

Seeing that his talks were having no effect, the Blood chief called a council of the young men. Both he and Crowfoot addressed them, telling them to stop going to war and to begin learning the white man's way of life. They discussed the possibility of making a peace treaty with the Gros Ventres, and enough support was gained that a treaty was enacted late in the spring.

This trip had a noticeable effect on the Blackfoot chief; although he still was weak, he seemed to have regained some of his old vitality. When he went back home, his interests turned again to the welfare of his tribe. He urged his people to farm if they wanted to earn a living, and encouraged them to start their own gardens. In May, a government official visiting the reserve saw many people working in the fields planting potatoes. And there among them was Crowfoot himself, with hoe in hand, working with his people. "You see the old chief hard at it," commented Agent Begg. "I believe you are the first white man that ever saw Crowfoot actively at work farming."[1]

During his visit, the official also saw a new house which the government had built for Crowfoot, but it was standing empty, for Crowfoot preferred his old lodge and had no use for the white man's building. Only when the winter came and his health failed would he seek the comfort of its snug interior.

By the winter of 1887–88, Crowfoot was almost continually sick and, even though he continued to work for his people's rights, he knew he was losing the battle for his own life. His trip to the Bloods had been a happy event, so he decided that his last days would be spent in traveling to the camps of the people he had known in the buffalo days—the Piegans, Gros Ventres, Bloods, and Sarcees. Like a dying monarch, he wanted

[1] William McGirr to Dewdney, May 25, 1887, No. 29689 in the Indian Affairs Archives.

to travel across the vast domain which had once been his and to look again upon the familiar faces of those he had seen on the open plains.

He set out on his first journey early in February, 1888, traveling with three oldtime companions, Three Bulls, Running Rabbit, and Medicine Shield. By the time they reached Fort Macleod, Crowfoot was so sick with erysipelas that he had to be confined to the Mounted Police hospital for the better part of a week. When he was released, he insisted that they go on. They stopped briefly at the Blood Reserve, where the chief recovered enough of his ebbing strength to move on to Montana. But by the time they crossed the border, he was in no condition to visit anyone and was taken directly to the Indian hospital at Badger Creek, where he stayed for several days until he was on his feet once more. Then, after only a few days of visiting, his party turned northward for home.

During the next four months, Crowfoot was bedridden most of the time, but by the end of July he felt well enough to try another trip. This time he went to the Piegans, who lived about a hundred miles away on the Oldman River. The visit was only for a few days, but nothing marred the journey and the chief enjoyed the companionship of his old friends. Heartened by his success, Crowfoot planned another trip in October to see the South Piegans once again. The weather was warm and dry for the whole trip south and by traveling slowly each day the chief passed through the Blood Reserve and reached the South Piegans in Montana without incident. Although he was weak from the journey, he enjoyed himself with warriors whom he had known in the old days. While there, the chief learned that the peace treaty between the Bloods and the Gros Ventres was being placed in constant jeopardy by young men from both sides stealing horses. The situation was further complicated by the fact that the Gros Ventres shared their reserve with the

Assiniboins, and, while the treaty included both tribes, the latter had been reluctant to sign.

Over the years Crowfoot had known several Assiniboin leaders, so, always the peacemaker, he announced his intention of visiting his old friends among the two Montana tribes. He was not strong enough for the ride, but the South Piegans provided a wagon and, with Medicine Shield taking the reins, the small party set out for the Fort Belknap Reservation. Others in the party included Three Bulls, Heavy Shoe, Bull Calf, and a few young men.

When they neared the reservation, the old chiefs came out to greet them and the Blackfeet were cordially welcomed to the camp. But as they approached the Assiniboin village, Crowfoot could sense the hostility of the younger men. As the handshaking continued, an Assiniboin warrior suddenly drew his whip and began lashing out at Crowfoot. Medicine Shield, who was sitting in the wagon beside Crowfoot, lunged in front of the old chief to protect him and cried out in pain as the whip cut off his little finger.

Everyone was stunned by the vicious outburst, and Heavy Shoe, who was the first to recover, angrily aimed his rifle at the heart of the young Assiniboin. Before he could fire, Crowfoot reached between them and placed his hand over the muzzle of the gun, while the Assiniboin chiefs led the young man away.

As they continued through the camp, Crowfoot was subjected to more insults. Women spat at him, young warriors made offensive signs, and everywhere there seemed to be hostility and hatred. The Blackfoot chief, though surprised by the reception, refused to leave until he was sure there was no hope for peace. Then the camp was stirred by the arrival of Black Bear, the Assiniboin head chief, who had been away on a hunting trip. On his return he was shocked by the way his

people had treated the Blackfoot delegation but found his
young warriors were too excited to listen to reason.

Riding over to the Blackfeet, the Assiniboin saw that Crowfoot's angry young men were ready to face death to revenge
the insults which had been heaped upon them. After a brief
consultation, Black Bear and Crowfoot stood side by side and
announced that if there were to be any fighting in the camp,
the two chiefs would have to be killed first; otherwise they
would join the tribe which was attacked and one man would
be fighting against his own people. The threat brought an
uneasy calm to the camp, and Crowfoot knew it was time to
leave before there were any further incidents. Sad, insulted,
and hurt, he made the painful trip back to the South Piegans
without seeing his old friends among the Gros Ventres. Not
until later did he learn that raids between the warring tribes
had ceased, partly through his bravery in facing up to the
Assiniboin warriors.

Crowfoot returned to Canada early in December with hu-
miliation and apparent failure added to his illness. He seldom
left his home during the winter and withdrew almost completely from the activities on the reserve.

In August, 1889, Crowfoot was ready to make another trip
to the South Piegans, but, to complicate his other ailments, his
vision became blurred. He was placed under a doctor's care
and his condition gradually improved, but his health was so
broken that he was not capable of making a long journey. Instead, in November he took a party of his followers on a visit
to the Sarcees, just west of Calgary. From there they went to
see the industrious Stonies, their onetime enemies, and, after
a few days there, they followed the old trail home, traveling
slowly for Crowfoot's sake.

On their way they saw the steel ribbon of railway tracks
which had brought such changes to their lives; they saw the

homesteads and ranches which dotted the old buffalo plains; they saw the towns and villages which had sprung up during the past few years. The Real People had become strangers in their own land and their only haven was in the sheltered valley at Blackfoot Crossing.

There Crowfoot went to die.

Early in April, 1890, he knew his time was drawing near. All winter he had been bedridden and his condition had continued to deteriorate. His only trip that spring would be to the Sand Hills, to that empty land where the Blackfoot spirits went after death.

His lodge was pitched on the prairie, a few yards from where the land dipped down to the valley of the Bow River. It was there the medicine men were called to perform their magic, sing their holy songs, and offer their prayers. With bells, drums, and whistles they were there to set up a constant clamor which would last day and night and drive away the evil spirits. Their chants had the wild rhythm of the warring days while they called upon the Sun for help. But day by day Crowfoot continued to weaken as his life slowly ebbed away.

When the chief's condition did not improve, Agent Begg sent for Doctor George, who arrived on April 22. With considerable difficulty the doctor persuaded the medicine men to stop their incantations while he checked the chief's condition and saw that he got some sleep. Two days later Crowfoot called his friends and relatives to his side. He told them to remain as friends to the white people, forget about the past, learn to work on their farms and make their living as the white man did. He thanked the government for the assistance it had given to his people and asked that a message be sent to Governor Dewdney expressing appreciation for his loyal friendship to the Blackfoot people.[2] Crowfoot then took a few mouthfuls of food, smoked his last pipe, and slipped into a coma.

At first his followers thought he was dead and a great cry of mourning arose from the lodge. But he had only drifted into that shadow world between life and death. He regained consciousness once during the afternoon and told his wives there should be no severing of fingers and scarring of their flesh when they mourned his passing. The next day, April 25, 1890, at three-thirty in the afternoon, the old chief died.

When his wailing widows stepped from the lodge, the men slowly drifted away to spread the news. "Men, women, children," shouted the camp announcer, "mourn over your great parent; you will no more hear his kind voice and its eloquent harangues. In your distress and misery, you will no more rush to his lodge for comfort and charities. He is no more. No one like him will fill his place."[3]

On the following day, the agency employees built a coffin seven feet long, three feet wide, and three feet deep, into which the chief's body was placed. On the lid, the name "Crowfoot" was spelled out in brass studs. The coffin had been made extra large so that the chief's personal possessions could be placed at his side for his trip to the Sand Hills. His tobacco, pipe, knife, blankets, and other objects all were beside his body as it lay

[2] Lacombe, "A Great Chieftain," *Macleod Gazette,* May 22 and 29, 1890.

[3] *Ibid.* In the article, Lacombe insisted that Crowfoot had died a Christian and "the fact that a clergyman of the Catholic church was officially attending the funeral, blessing and reciting the prayers over the grave, proves [this] conclusively." There can be no doubt that a baptism took place, for the record of it exists in the Roman Catholic mission. It states "that Joseph Crowfoot (Sapo omarxika), 65 years old, was baptized on the 23rd day of April 1890, according to the Rites of the Roman Catholic Church, at Blackfoot Reserve, Cluny, Alta., by Rev. Fr. Doucet, O.M.I."

However, Protestant missionaries disagreed. "He died as he had lived," wrote J. W. Tims in the *Calgary Daily Herald,* April 29, 1933, "in the faith of his fathers. His favorite horse was shot at his death, so that he might ride it in the 'happy hunting grounds.'" Informants say that Crowfoot was not buried inside the little Catholic cemetery but just outside its southern fence. In about 1927 the cemetery was repaired and the fence extended to include the graves of Three Bulls and Crowfoot.

in state. On the afternoon of the twenty-sixth, Father Doucet read the burial service beside the little Catholic cemetery, while crowds of Indians and white employees gathered around. Men and women wept and wailed as they walked from their lodges to the chief's last resting place.

One Blackfoot Indian who was six years old at the time remembered the funeral well.

> We were camped along the Bow River, and everyone was gathered for the funeral. As we were walking up the hill to join the crowd, we saw a man named Far Away Voice, who was wearing only a breech cloth and was wailing and mourning for the loss of Crowfoot. He cried out that the Blackfoot were sorry to see him go and they missed him. At the top of the hill were more people mourning, wives, relatives and many others. The old man's wailing affected us so much that we joined him and began to cry.[4]

The Indian agent wanted to bury Crowfoot under the ground like a white man, but the Blackfeet refused; they insisted he be placed above the ground like an Indian. Finally, in a compromise, a grave was dug so that part of the coffin was below the surface and part of it was above, and a small log house was built over it for protection.

Word of Crowfoot's death spread across the continent and over the seas. From all parts of the world regrets were expressed over the passing of the great chief. Governor Dewdney, who had become minister of the interior; Sir John A. Macdonald, the prime minister; leading statesmen; Mounted Policemen; missionaries; and old acquaintances all were grieved by the news.

Crowfoot's appearance, actions, and wisdom had captured the imagination of the white population. His proud bearing,

[4] Interview with One Gun, March 5, 1957.

colorful regalia, and lean hawklike face fitted perfectly into the white man's idea of a great chief. He had been a warrior, a peacemaker, an orator, and a diplomat. Crowfoot had been the father of his people, the great chief of the Blackfeet. His old friend Edgar Dewdney stated:

> The demise of Chief Crowfoot, the Chief of the Blackfoot Tribe . . . has left a blank which it will be difficult, if not impossible, to fill. . . . Crowfoot died as he had lived, loyal and true to the "Great Mother"—almost with his last breath exhorting his people to be obedient to the authorities. He was a remarkable man, considering the circumstances in which his lot was cast; and never was his force of character more clearly demonstrated than when he saw that the day of the tomahawk and scalping knife was over, and that the era for the cultivation, by his people, of all that would tend to peace and prosperity, had set in. The same energy and tact that he had so often displayed on the battlefield and in the council meeting were now shown in counselling his people and influencing them in their endeavours to abandon their old habits and to conform themselves to the new order of things; and well did he succeed, for a more loyal tribe of Indians cannot be found in the North-West than the Blackfeet, as was well demonstrated by their refusal to join in the Half-breed rebellion of 1885, though frequently importuned by the Indian allies of the rebels to do so. Crowfoot died beloved by his people, feared by his foes, esteemed by all.[5]

Dewdney's prediction that Crowfoot's vacancy would be almost impossible to fill was correct. The head chieftainship was taken by his foster brother, Three Bulls, who, without the guidance of his leader, proved to be incapable of handling the responsibilities of the high office. In the passing years other

[5] *Annual Report of the Department of Indian Affairs for the Year Ended 31st December, 1890*, xxix-xxx.

head chiefs took his place, including a grandson of Crowfoot, but none was able to replace him in effective leadership.

He was a man of his era, successfully leading his people from a nomadic life to their reserve without bloodshed. Other tribes, in both Canada and the United States, which tried to block the inevitable movement of the white men by resorting to war won no lasting battles. Perhaps there was a feeling of bravery and independence in wiping out the white invaders, but the tribe eventually paid a huge price. Crowfoot, in the fortunate position of knowing the white man's far-reaching strength, chose to greet him as a friend and to extract from him the best possible terms for the inevitable future. That he succeeded was evident by the way the government treated his tribe for many years after the rebellion. While those who were involved in the Riel rebellion often were oppressed and ignored, the Blackfeet showed steady progress as they developed as ranchers, farmers, and coal miners. Like the Bloods and Piegans to the south, they could always claim they had kept the treaty and expected the government to do the same. And for this they could thank Crowfoot, their great chief.